How To Use This Study Guide

This 15-lesson study guide corresponds to *"How To Keep Your Head on Straight in a World Gone Crazy" With Rick Renner* (Renner TV). Each lesson in this study guide covers a topic that is addressed during the program series, with questions and references supplied to draw you deeper into your own private study of the Scriptures on this subject.

To derive the most benefit from this study guide, consider the following:

First, watch or listen to the program prior to working through the corresponding lesson in this guide. (Programs can also be viewed at **renner.org** by clicking on the Media/Archives links or on our Renner Ministries YouTube channel.)

Second, take the time to look up the scriptures included in each lesson. Prayerfully consider their application to your own life.

Third, use a journal or notebook to make note of your answers to each lesson's Study Questions and Practical Application challenges.

Fourth, invest specific time in prayer and in the Word of God to consult with the Holy Spirit. Write down the scriptures or insights He reveals to you.

Finally, take action! Whatever the Lord tells you to do according to His Word, do it.

For added insights on this subject, it is recommended that you obtain Rick Renner's book *How To Keep Your Head on Straight in a World Gone Crazy* You may also select from Rick's other available resources by placing your order at **renner.org** or by calling 1-800-742-5593.

TOPIC

Prophecies About Error in the Church in the Last Days

SCRIPTURES

1. **1 Timothy 4:1** — Now the Spirit speaketh expressly, that in the latter times some shall depart from the faith, giving heed to seducing spirits and doctrines of demons.

GREEK WORDS

1. "speaketh expressly" — ῥητῶς (*rhetos*): unmistakably; vividly; pictures something spoken clearly or something that is unquestionable, certain, and sure

2. "latter" — ὕστερος (*husteros*): later; pictures the ultimate end or the very last of **something**

3. "times" — καιρός (*kairos*): a season

4. "depart" — ἀφίστημι (*aphistemi*): a compound of ἀπό (*apo*) and ἵστημι (*histimi*); ἀπό (*apo*) means away, and ἵστημι (*histimi*) means to stand; compounded, they form the word ἀφίστημι (*aphistemi*), which means to stand apart from; to distance one's self from; to step away from; to withdraw from; or to shrink away from; it is from this very Greek word that we derive the word apostate or apostasy

5. "the faith" — πίστεως (*pisteos*): refers to doctrine or to the long-held, time-tested teachings of Scripture

6. "giving heed" — προσέχω (*prosecho*): to embrace

7. "seducing" — πλανάω (*planao*): to wander; pictures deception or a moral wandering; depicts a person (or nation) that has veered from a solid path; as a result of veering morally, this person is adrift; also used to depict a lost animal that cannot find its path; to morally lose one's bearings; to wander off course

8. "doctrines" — διδασκαλία (*didaskalia*): well-packaged teaching that is applicable to lifestyle

A Note From Rick Renner

I am on a personal quest to see a "revival of the Bible" so people can establish their lives on a firm foundation that will stand strong and endure the test as the end-time storm winds begin to intensify.

In order to experience a revival of the Bible in your personal life, it is important to take time each day to read, receive, and apply its truths to your life. James tells us that if we will continue in the perfect law of liberty — refusing to be forgetful hearers but determined to be doers — we will be blessed in our ways. As you watch or listen to the programs in this series and work through this corresponding study guide, I trust that you will search the Scriptures and allow the Holy Spirit to help you hear something new from God's Word that applies specifically to your life. I encourage you to be a doer of the Word that He reveals to you. Whatever the cost, I assure you — it will be worth it.

> Thy words were found, and I did eat them;
> and thy word was unto me the joy and rejoicing of mine heart:
> for I am called by thy name, O Lord God of hosts.
> — Jeremiah 15:16

Your brother and friend in Jesus Christ,

Rick Renner

Rick Renner

How To Keep Your Head on Straight in a World Gone Crazy

9. "demons" — δαιμόνιον (*daimonion*): in context, evil spirits, demons, devils; the ancient world generally believed demons thickly populated the lower regions of the air and that spirits were the primary cause of disasters, suffering, and actions of insanity

SYNOPSIS

The 15 lessons in this study on *How To Keep Your Head on Straight in a World Gone Crazy* will focus on the following topics:

- Prophecies About Error in the Church in the Last Days
- What Jesus Said About Error at the End of the Age
- Spiritual Smugglers
- Contending for the Faith in the Last Days
- How To Pray for Leaders Who Are in Error
- Timothy's Situation with Erring Leaders
- The Real Problem: Lack of Bible Knowledge
- How To Judge if a Teaching Is Good or Bad
- The Goal of Good Teaching
- What Happens When Someone Swerves From the Truth
- Seducing Spirits and Doctrines of Demons
- Placing a Fixed Foundation Under People's Lives
- How To Be a Good Minister of Jesus Christ
- The Right Spiritual Diet
- Old Wives Tales and Fables

When the apostle Paul returned to Ephesus, he entered the city through the interior roadways, walking through the Magnesia Gate and traveling down the Magnesia Road. On his left and his right, beautiful columns lined the street upon which sat numerous idols vividly painted in life-like colors. Ephesus was a very dark place spiritually, but with the empowerment of the Holy Spirit and the help of his friends Aquila and Priscilla, Paul established a church in the heart of this pagan city. When it was time for him to move on, Paul installed Timothy to be the pastor of this church. Many years later, he wrote to Timothy and prophesied what was going to take place at the very end of the last days.

The emphasis of this lesson:

At the very end of the age — the time in which we are now living — the Holy Spirit has informed us that a worldwide departure from the time-tested truths of Scripture would take place.

A Prophetic Warning for the Last Days

The Early Church was born into a world of paganism where there were many types of demonic activity and the worship of false gods. Out of this wicked environment, many strange doctrines of demons began to circulate. Yet as troubling and perverse as things were, the apostle Paul warned Timothy — *and us* — of what would happen in the very last of the last days.

In First Timothy 4:1, Paul said, "Now the Spirit speaketh expressly, that in the latter times some shall depart from the faith, giving heed to seducing spirits and doctrines of demons." The Holy Spirit, speaking through Paul, prophetically pointed His finger 2,000 years into the future and told us what would take place.

First, notice the phrase "speaketh expressly." It is the Greek word *rhetos*, and it means unmistakably; vividly. It pictures *something spoken clearly or something that is unquestionable, certain, and sure.* By using the word *rhetos*, the Holy Spirit makes His point unequivocally clear: The events He is about to describe are not a possibility; they are definite and will surely come to pass.

Next, notice the words "latter times." The word "latter" is the Greek word *husteros*, which means *later*, and it pictures *the ultimate end or the very last of something.* By using this word, the Holy Spirit is pointing to the very end of the age — to a time when there is virtually no more time remaining.

The word "times" is also important. It is the Greek word *kairos*, and it describes *a season.* When you join these two words together — *husteros kairos*, translated here as "latter times" — they describe *the very last season or period of the Church age.* With this understanding, we can know with certainty one of the major signs that we are living in the very end of the age.

A Great Departure Is Imminent

Speaking futuristically, the Holy Spirit said, "…In the latter times some shall depart from the faith…" (1 Timothy 4:1). Understanding the word "depart" in this verse is vital. It is the Greek word *aphistemi*, which is a compound of the words *apo* and *histimi*. The word *apo* means *away*, and the word *histimi* means *to stand*. When these words are compounded, they form the word *aphistemi*, which means *to stand apart from; to distance one's self from; to step away from; to withdraw from; or to shrink away from.* It is from this very Greek word that we derive the word "apostate" or "apostasy."

Thus, when the Holy Spirit says that "some shall *depart* from the faith," He is describing a very gradual withdrawal that takes place slowly over a period of time. This is the picture of a person who changes the position of what he or she once believed, little by little. The departure is so gradual that those who are in the process of withdrawing may not even realize it is happening.

To be clear, this departure is not a rejection of faith. That is, it is not a blatant, outright denunciation of one's belief. It is a gradual, step-by-step move away from what one once believed toward something different. It is a very subtle, almost imperceptible departure as it is occurring. This is an occurrence that is imminent in these last of the last days.

What Does It Mean To Stray From the Faith?

The Bible says that the departure that will take place will be from "the faith." The phrase "the faith" is the Greek word *pisteos*, and it specifically refers to *doctrine or the long-held, time-tested teachings of Scripture*. The Greek here includes the definite article, which means the departure is not from faith in miracles or faith in healing, per se. Rather, it is a slow drift from "the faith" in Christ.

This means that at the very end of the age, there will be some believers who will depart from the clear teaching of the Scripture. Little by little, they will distance themselves from God's truth and embrace something new that has captured their attention.

Thankfully, the Bible doesn't say everyone will depart from the faith; it just says that *some* will. Although it will be a noticeable number of people, many others will press into the faith and become more deeply grounded in the Word.

Again, this verse doesn't say people will *reject* the faith. It says they will *depart*, or *stray*, from the faith. Rejecting is abrupt and deliberate — departing is slow and is usually unintentional. There is a huge difference between the two, but that is why the Holy Spirit urges us to be on guard against this "phenomenon" of deception that will sweep over society like a tsunami in the very last days.

Why Some Will Depart — Identifying the Source

The reason some will depart from the faith is the result of "…giving heed to seducing spirits and doctrines of demons" (1 Timothy 4:1). The phrase "giving heed" is the Greek word *prosecho*. It is the compound of two words: the word *pros*, which means *to lean toward*, and the word *echo*, which means *to hold or to embrace*. When the words *pros* and *echo* are joined to form the word *prosecho*, it pictures *a person who has believed one thing for a very long time now leaning in a new direction believing something else*. Slowly but surely, they have released and withdrawn from what they once held precious and dear and have begun to hold on to new ideas and new systems of belief.

This leads us to ask the question: What is influencing these individuals to change their position and leave the clear teaching of Scripture? Through Paul, the Holy Spirit identifies the cause as "seducing spirits and doctrines of demons." The word "seducing" is the Greek word *planao*, which means *to wander*. It pictures *deception or a moral wandering*. It depicts *a person (or nation) that has veered from a solid path, and as a result of veering morally, this person is adrift*. The word *planao* is also used to depict *a lost animal that cannot find its path*. Furthermore, it means *to morally lose one's bearings; to wander off course*.

Without question, this describes with great accuracy much of the senseless thinking and behavior we are seeing in society today. Many people have lost their sense of what is right and wrong just as the prophet Isaiah foretold thousands of years ago when he said, "Woe unto them that call evil good, and good evil…" (Isaiah 5:20).

Again, Paul identified the source of the problem as "seducing spirits and doctrines of demons." The word "doctrines" in First Timothy 4:1 is the Greek word *didaskalia*, and it describes *a well-packaged teaching that is applicable to a lifestyle*. Thus, when it is presented, the error will sound logical and appeal to one's flesh. People will hear it and say, "Wow! That's a possibility I should consider."

Make no mistake. Behind these well-packaged systems of thought that are being promoted are "demons." The word "demons" is the Greek word *daimonion*, which in context, describes *evil spirits, demons, devils*. The ancient world generally believed demons thickly populated the lower regions of the air and that spirits were the primary cause of disasters, suffering, and actions of insanity.

How Can You Avoid the Moral Meltdown?

In these last of the last days, there is going to be widespread deception induced on a societal scale greater than ever before, and the source of the mayhem will be demonic spirits. The Holy Spirit makes this crystal clear in First Timothy 4:1 as well as in many other passages of the New Testament.

This infiltration of seducing spirits and doctrines of demons was not prophesied to scare us, but rather to *prepare* us and help us prevent those who are part of the Church from being beguiled. God is never interested in scaring His people, but He is very interested in warning us when danger is on the horizon. The Holy Spirit sounded this alarm to prevent error from ever finding entrance into our churches, our personal lives, or the lives of our children and grandchildren.

Therefore, in order to keep your head on straight in a world gone crazy, you really need to press into the timeless, unchanging truth of God's Word. Intimately knowing the Word and the Holy Spirit who authored it will serve to guard your heart and mind from the deceptive doctrine of demons. It will give you the stability you need to stand and protect yourself and those you love from departing from the faith.

STUDY QUESTIONS

Study to shew thyself approved unto God, a workman that needeth not to be ashamed, rightly dividing the word of truth.
— 2 Timothy 2:15

1. Without question, being grounded in the Word of God is a vital and valuable deterrent to keep us from departing from the faith. Carefully reflect on these verses and identify the life-giving qualities they reveal about Scripture.
    - Psalm 119:89; Isaiah 40:8; Matthew 24:35; and 1 Peter 1:25

- Psalm 119:9; John 17:17
- Hebrews 4:12; James 1:21; and Romans 1:16

What is the Holy Spirit speaking to you as you read through these truths?

2. Explain the difference between departing from the faith and outrightly rejecting the faith.

PRACTICAL APPLICATION

**But be ye doers of the word, and not hearers only,
deceiving your own selves.
—James 1:22**

The word "depart" in First timothy 4:1 is the Greek word *aphistemi*, which means *to stand apart from; to distance one's self from; to step away from; to withdraw from; or to shrink away from.* This departure is a gradual withdrawal that takes place slowly over a period of time — a subtle, step-by-step move away from what one once believed toward something different.

Take a moment to pray and ask the Lord these important questions and then listen for His answers.

1. "Lord, have I fallen into this subtle, almost imperceptible pattern of *departure*? Am I unknowingly being influenced by seducing spirits and *morally wandering*?"

2. "If I have, where am I adrift? In what specific ways have my beliefs changed?"

3. "Lord, please forgive me. Show me what I can do to stay anchored in the truth of Your Word and help my loved ones do the same, in Jesus' name."

TOPIC

What Jesus Said About Error at the End of the Age

SCRIPTURES

1. **1 Timothy 4:1** — Now the Spirit speaketh expressly, that in the latter times some shall depart from the faith, giving heed to seducing spirits and doctrines of demons.
2. **Matthew 24:4** — ...Take heed that no man deceive you.
3. **2 Thessalonians 2:7** — For the mystery of iniquity doth already work: only he who now letteth will let, until he be taken out of the way.

GREEK WORDS

1. "deceive"/"delusion" — πλανάω (*planao*): to wander; pictures deception or a moral wandering; depicts a person (or nation) that has veered from a solid path; as a result of veering morally, this person is adrift; also used to depict a lost animal that cannot find its path; to morally lose one's bearings; to wander off course

SYNOPSIS

The Magnesia Road is very important to our Christian history. It was the highway Paul traveled when he reentered the city of Ephesus and met a group of disciples he led to Christ and then prayed that they might receive the baptism of the Holy Spirit (*see* Acts 19:1-7). The salvation of these 12 men was the catalyst that launched a mighty move of God in the upper part of Ephesus. Within three years, the Church was booming all across the city.

When it was time for Paul to leave, he appointed Timothy as the pastor of this local church. Years later, he wrote Timothy and prophesied of what was coming in the last days. He said, "Now the Spirit speaketh expressly, that in the latter times some shall depart from the faith, giving heed to seducing spirits and doctrines of demons" (1 Timothy 4:1).

Interestingly, the apostle Peter echoed a very similar warning in Second Peter 2:1 when he said, "But there were false prophets also among the people, even as there shall be false teachers among you…." This foretelling of an invasion of error in the Church in the Last Days was not only voiced by Peter and Paul, but also by Jesus as we will see in this lesson.

The emphasis of this lesson:

We're living in the last of the last days, and the Bible emphatically teaches that deception will abound. Therefore, we need to be alert and awake, taking heed that we are not deceived.

The Essence of the Holy Spirit's Warning Through Paul

In First Timothy 4:1, the apostle Paul wrote to Timothy and said, "Now the Spirit speaketh expressly, that in the latter times some shall depart from the faith, giving heed to seducing spirits and doctrines of demons." We learned in our last lesson that the phrase "speaketh expressly" is the Greek word *rhetos*, which means *something spoken clearly or something that is unquestionable, certain, and sure*. Thus, what the Holy Spirit "expressly" said is definitely going to take place.

Using the most emphatic language of the Greek, the Holy Spirit warned believers of all generations everywhere that at the very end of the age — the last season of time — demonic spirits would package and propagate false teachings that would be so enticing, it would cause a number of believers to gradually turn away from the truth of Scripture they previously embraced and held dear, and begin leaning toward new, ungodly doctrines.

To ensure that we hear and heed this warning, the Holy Spirit reiterated it in many other passages of the New Testament, including Second Timothy 4:3 and 4, Second Thessalonians 2:1-12, and the words of Jesus recorded in Matthew 24.

The Foremost 'Sign' Jesus Gave for the End of the Age

Toward the end of Jesus' ministry, the disciples approached Him with questions that many believers are still seeking answers for today. The Bible says, "And as he [Jesus] sat upon the mount of Olives, the disciples came unto him privately, saying, Tell us, when shall these things be? And what shall be the sign of thy coming, and of the end of the world?" (Matthew 24:3).

Notice the word "sign" in this verse. It is the Greek word *semeion*, which is translated from the Greek word that is used to describe *signposts* that helped travelers know exactly where they were as they made their way to their destinations. In effect, the disciples wanted to know what the "signposts" would be that would confirm we've finally reached the very end of the age.

Jesus spoke of many signs that would precede the end of the age, including signs in the heavens, economic instability, great seismic activity, legal prosecution of Christians, warring political systems, famines, persecution, pestilences, commotions, ethnic conflicts, imprisonment of believers, the emergence of false prophets, the love of many waxing cold, fearful sights, unknown diseases, wars and rumors of wars.

Jesus predicted all of these things would be signs, but *the first and foremost* sign He provided was a warning that a worldwide deception would emerge at the very end of the age. In Matthew 24:4, He said, "…Take heed that no man deceive you." In other words, Jesus was saying, "Above everything else, the most telling sign to let you know that you have entered the very end of the age is a widespread, worldwide deception." This warning was to all His disciples — then and now.

'Take Heed That No Man Deceive You'

The phrase "take heed" is the Greek word *blepo*, which in Matthew 24:4 was intended to jar and jolt the disciples to be alert and pay close attention to what Jesus was about to say. It was the equivalent of His saying, "Listen up, guys! I have something extremely important to tell you. If you really want to know what will be the sign of the very end of the age, wake up and listen to what I'm about to say." This is what is embodied in the phrase "take heed."

He then said, "Don't let any man *deceive* you." The word "deceive" in Matthew 24:4 is the Greek word *planao* — the same Greek word translated as "seducing" in First Timothy 4:1. The word *planao* means *to wander off course*; *to morally lose one's bearings*. It pictures *deception or a moral wandering*. It depicts *a person (or nation) that has veered from a solid path.*

As a result of veering morally, this person is adrift. The word *planao* is also used to describe *a lost animal that cannot find its path.*

When Jesus said, "Take heed that no man deceive you," He was prophesying that at the end of the age, many in society would leave the clear teachings of Scripture, which is a moral, righteous path, and begin to morally drift into deception. In fact, they would stray so far from the truth that they would be like a lost animal that cannot find its way back home.

The word "deceive" not only depicts the behavior of someone who once walked on a solid path and has wandered off, but it also pictures someone who is drifting and teetering on the edge of a treacherous route. He or she is now going against the grain of everything that was once his or her core beliefs. The course this individual is on is unreliable, unpredictable, and even dangerous.

This level of deception and departure from time-tested beliefs and traditions that are based on biblical values is what we can expect to see on a worldwide scale at the very end of the age. The truth is, it is already here.

A Strong Delusion Is Upon Us

The spirit of this world is working furiously to eliminate every trace of a godly foundation and replace it with a last-days deception that will ultimately usher in a season when the antichrist rules the lost world for the final period of time. If you are spiritually sensitive, you are aware that this process is already underway. There is an onslaught of deception that is attacking culture from every direction. It is a mindset that is seeping into our government, education system, and virtually all forms of art and media.

Under the inspiration of the Holy Spirit, the apostle Paul prophesied in Second Thessalonians 2:11 that at the end of the age, there would be a worldwide mutiny against God. This would be the precursor to Christ's return. The words Paul used to describe this mutiny are "strong delusion." In other words, a vast majority of the populace would become so seduced, duped, and beguiled that they would throw off the time-tested law of God. That is what is meant by the word "delusion." The Bible says this would be the result of the "mystery of iniquity" already at work in the world (*see* 2 Thessalonians 2:7).

This lets us know that there has been a secret, sinister plan orchestrated by Satan and his demonic forces to slowly but surely walk the world into deception. Gradually, almost imperceptibly, the devil has been trying to modify the thinking of the world to prepare it to produce and then embrace a man of lawlessness to lead them. The Bible calls this lawless man the "antichrist." A lawless world will readily receive this man of lawlessness.

How can we keep our head on straight in a world that is leaning toward lawlessness? The answer is to live our lives according to the Word of God. Although the world is sinking into depravity, we have been called to and equipped for a higher walk — a walk that is grounded in the Word and guided by the Holy Spirit.

STUDY QUESTIONS

Study to shew thyself approved unto God, a workman that needeth not to be ashamed, rightly dividing the word of truth.
— 2 Timothy 2:15

Ultimately, the enemy is trying to produce a lawless society and a lawless leader he can fully control and take in the direction of destruction. The apostle John wrote about this man of lawlessness in First John 2:18-26.

1. Carefully read this passage and identify the name and characteristics given to this man.

2. What does John say God has given to you to protect you from being sucked into error?

3. How does this passage in First John connect with Jesus' words in John 16:13 and 14? Who is at work and what is He specifically doing?

4. What is your part in receiving this protection? Are you doing it?

PRACTICAL APPLICATION

But be ye doers of the word, and not hearers only, deceiving your own selves.
— James 1:22

1. Isaiah prophesied about the great deception that would engulf society, saying, "Woe unto them that call evil good, and good evil; that put darkness for light, and light for darkness..." (Isaiah 5:20). What

real-life examples of this insanity and gross confusion in society today can you identify? (Consider our education system, government, the courtrooms, and the entertainment industry.)

2. It is certainly true that believers of *every* time period have had to deal with issues of moral degradation and societal ills in the world around them. So how do you think this end-time deception and deprivation differs from previous generations?

LESSON 3

TOPIC

Spiritual Smugglers

SCRIPTURES

1. **2 Peter 2:1** — But there were false prophets among the people, even as there shall be false teachers among you, who privily shall bring in damnable heresies, even denying the Lord that bought them, and bring upon themselves swift destruction.

GREEK WORDS

1. "false teachers" — ψευδοδιδάσκαλος (*pseudodidaskalos*): a compound of ψευδής (*pseudes*) and διδάσκαλος (*didaskalos*); ψευδής (*pseudes*) carries the idea of any type of falsehood; pictures one who projects an image of himself that's false or of one who walks in pretense or intentionally misrepresents facts or truths; διδάσκαλος (*didaskalos*) pictures a masterful teacher; when compounded, ψευδοδιδάσκαλος (*pseudodidaskalos*) depicts teachers who may have begun as authentic, God-called teachers, but who over a period of time have progressively veered off course

2. "privily shall bring in" — παρεισάγω (*pareisago*): a compound of three Greek words: παρά (*para*), which means alongside; εἰς (*eis*), which means into; and ἄγω (*ago*), which means to lead; the word παρά (*para*) in this context indicates that the false teachers Peter referenced will walk alongside other believers; the word εἰς (*eis*) means they will bring their false doctrine right into the church; the word ἄγω (*ago*) suggests that these individuals will hold positions of leadership in the church;

compounded, as in Second Peter 2:1, **παρεισάγω** (*pareisago*) denotes a smuggler attempting to covertly transport illegal contraband across a border while using a disguise, or stealth, to conceal his activities

3. "heresies" — **αἵρεσις** (*hairesis*): choice or opinion; in context, false doctrines or false teachings; a particular school of thought

4. "damnable" — **ἀπώλεια** (*apoleia*): destruction; something that is destroyed, decayed, rotten, or ruined; by using this word, the apostle clearly spelled out what the doctrine of compromise would produce if it wasn't stopped — destruction and devastation

5. "bought" — **ἀγοράζω** (*agoradzo*): to purchase; from the New Testament word for redemption

6. "Lord" — **δεσπότη** (*despotes*): an administrative term normally referring to a CEO or to one who has authority over others, especially over others in the executive department directly under his control

7. "denying" — **ἀρνέομαι** (*arneomai*): to knowingly deny; to knowingly disown; to knowingly reject; to knowingly refuse; or to knowingly renounce; depicts something done with one's full consent and understanding of what he or she is doing

8. "swift" — **ταχινός** (*tachinos*): swift; sudden; quick

9. "destruction" — **ἀπώλεια** (*apoleia*): something that is destroyed, decayed, rotten, or ruined; devastation

SYNOPSIS

Located in the ancient city of Ephesus was a place called Domitian Square, and in the very center of that square stood the Temple of Domitian. Its ruins are still visible today. The construction for this shrine was initiated by Vespasian, Domitian's father, and was originally built in honor of the Flavian dynasty of which they were all a part. However, after Vespasian's death and the death of Titus who followed him as emperor for a brief time, Domitian inherited the throne and turned the project into a temple dedicated to himself. He was a demented leader who declared himself to be god and then established an entire religion, which included a full priesthood and rituals of worship. The Temple of Domitian is a symbol of the dark evil that was spreading across the Roman Empire.

During that same period of darkness, the Spirit of God had established a powerful church in the city of Ephesus through the work of the apostle Paul and his co-laborers Aquila and Priscilla. In spite of great suffering throughout the wicked reigns of Domitian, Titus, and Nero, this body of believers was thriving. When the apostle Paul was chased out of town due to persecution (*see* Acts 20), he was unable to adequately say goodbye to the church elders, so he asked them to meet him in Miletus. When they arrived, he prophesied what would take place inside the church of Ephesus. He said, "For I know this, that after my departing shall grievous wolves enter in among you, not sparing the flock" (Acts 20:29). The Holy Spirit was warning the leaders of what the enemy was going to attempt to do so that they would prepare and protect themselves from error infiltrating the church. It is the same type of warning He is giving us today.

Throughout the New Testament, the Holy Spirit has spoken about the end times, revealing the condition of the world, the Church, as well as the hearts of people. He has told us what will take place in order to prepare us to deal with the challenges we are presently facing. We've learned in our previous lesson that "seducing spirits" and "doctrines of devils" will mislead many, causing a slow departure from the timeless truth of Scripture (*see* 1 Timothy 4:1). The apostle Paul was not the only one who wrote about this. Peter also commented on what was going to take place in the Last Days.

The emphasis of this lesson:

In these last days, there will be false teachers who are consciously trying to smuggle error into the Church. They once walked in relationship with the Lord, but have since given place to a doctrine of compromise and rejected the Lord's correction. Destruction awaits them.

What *Was* Will Be Again

In Second Peter 2:1, Peter said, "There were false prophets among the people, even as there shall be false teachers among you, who privily shall bring in damnable heresies, even denying the Lord that bought them, and bring upon themselves swift destruction." In this passage, Peter began by talking about the past, saying that there *were* false prophets within the Church. Then he speaks futuristically — pointing to the end of the Church age — saying there *shall be* false teachers among you once again.

Notice the phrase "false teachers." It is the Greek word *pseudodidaskalos*, which is a compound of two words. The first word is *pseudes*, which carries *the idea of any type of falsehood and pictures one who projects an* image of himself that's false or of one who walks in pretense or intentionally misrepresents facts or truths. The second word is *didaskalos*, which describes a *masterful teacher*. When *pseudes* and *didaskalos* are compounded to form the word *pseudodidaskalos*, it depicts *teachers who may have begun as authentic, God-called teachers, but who over a period of time have progressively veered off course*. The message they now offer is counterfeit.

During the time Peter wrote this, the Church was already dealing with the problem of false teachers (*pseudodidaskalos*). Ironically, the counterfeit message they were peddling then is the same counterfeit message that is being propagating now. They were teaching a doctrine of *compromise*. In effect, they were saying, "Let's not be so strict and live separate from the world. If we'll relax our beliefs and be more inclusive, we can blend together with society." But in order to compromise, they had to water down Scripture and move away from its solid, time-tested teaching. This is exactly what is happening today.

There are false teachers currently in the Church who are modifying the Bible to make it say what they want it to say. This bending of truth serves to accommodate ungodly lifestyles and make people comfortable in their sin. Some are preaching and teaching a version of the Bible that is so far from the truth, it celebrates behaviors that are clearly forbidden in Scripture. This is a blatant departure from the truth. Any "new," "cutting-edge," or "progressive" theological concepts, ideas, or systems of thought that contradict the truth of God's Word is a doctrine of demons — regardless of how sophisticated it's packaged or how polished the messenger is.

False Teachers Will Smuggle in Counterfeit Truth

Peter went on to say that these false teachers "…privily shall bring in damnable heresies." In the Greek, this phrase is a compound of three words — the words *para*, *eis*, and *ago*. The word *para* means *alongside*; the word *eis* means *into*; and the word *ago* means *to lead*. In this context, the word *para* indicates that the false teachers Peter referenced will walk *alongside other believers*; the word *eis* means *they will bring their false doctrine right into the church*; and the word *ago* suggests that *these individuals will hold positions of leadership in the church*. When all three words are compounded to form the word *pareisago*, it denotes *a smuggler attempting to covertly transport illegal contraband across a border while using a disguise, or stealth, to conceal his activities.*

This meaning clearly shows that these people know what they're doing. They fully realize that what they are teaching is a departure from Scripture. But instead of presenting their doctrine as a departure from truth, they are disguising it and smuggling it into the Church. The word *pareisago* depicts *a conscious effort* — at least on the part of the seducing spirits who are behind the deception — to sneak error into the Church in a veiled way to prevent it from being detected.

It's important to note that some of these false teachers fully believe and embrace the error they're peddling. They have swallowed the lie and believe it wholeheartedly. As a result, deception is at work in and through their lives. Theses spiritual smugglers so cleverly lay truth *alongside (para)* error that it makes the error very difficult to detect. This is especially dangerous for new, immature believers who don't know the Scripture. When they see truth and error laying side-by-side, they cannot discern which one is right and which is wrong. Consequently, they accept all of it as truth.

The Bible Calls It 'Damnable Heresies'

Second Peter 2:1 identifies the lies being smuggled into the Church as "damnable heresies." The word "heresies" is the Greek word *hairesis*, which simply means *choice or opinion*. In Greek culture, it described *a particular school of thought*. On its own, the word *hairesis* isn't bad. However, in the context of this verse, it indicates *false doctrines or false teachings*. It is something considered to be *foul, evil, or heretical*. To be clear, *heretical* teaching is *any belief or doctrine that is divergent from the beliefs presented in Scripture*. Beliefs or principles that line up or agree with the teaching of the New Testament are referred to as *orthodox doctrines*.

This brings us to the word "damnable," which in Greek is the word *apoleia*. This word describes *destruction; something that is destroyed, decayed, rotten, or ruined*. By using the word *apoleia*, the apostle Peter clearly spelled out what the doctrine of compromise would produce if it wasn't stopped — *destruction and devastation*. Thus, Peter was raising his voice and sounding an alarm to believers everywhere in all generations not to embrace the doctrine of compromise, as it will lead to a path of destruction and devastation and create a weak, impotent version of the Church.

When you read Second Peter 2:1 in the Greek, it actually reverses the sentence structure. Instead of saying "damnable heresies" as we read it in the *King James Version*, it says "heresies damnable." This implies that the error being taught was a school of divergent thinking, which produced damnation and devastation to those who embraced it. The same consequences hold true for us today. If we embrace "damnable heresies," it will produce ruin and destruction in our lives.

These False Prophets Were Once Believers

The apostle Peter went on to say that these false prophets — both in his day and in ours — would even deny "...the Lord that bought them, and bring upon themselves swift destruction" (2 Peter 2:1). The word "bought" in this verse is very important, as it lets us know that these false teachers are *insiders*, not outsiders. In Greek, the word "bought" is *agoradzo*, which means *to purchase*. It is from the New Testament word for *redemption*. In other words, these spiritual smugglers were *redeemed individuals* who began their journey of faith as authentic Christians. However, over a period of time, they listened to seducing spirits and were led off course. They then began to teach others the same divergent truth that they had begun to believe.

Peter noted that these compromised Christians would be "denying the Lord that bought them." The word "Lord" here is the Greek word *despotes*. Usually, the Greek word used for "Lord" is the word *Kurios*, which means *supreme master and Lord*. The word *despotes* is very different in that it is *an administrative term normally referring to a CEO or to one who has authority over others, especially over others in the executive department directly under his control*. By using the term *despotes*, the Holy Spirit is telling us that these false teachers were once called and installed by Christ to serve in the administrative wing of the Church — that is, the fivefold ministry (*see* Ephesians 4:11). But after being poisoned by erroneous doctrine, they actually began denying the correction of Christ.

The word "denying" is the Greek word *arneomai*, which means *to knowingly deny; to knowingly disown; to knowingly reject; to knowingly refuse; or to knowingly renounce*. This word depicts *something done with one's full consent and understanding of what he or she is doing*. The use of this word actually reveals the faithfulness of God to His people. If a person is in error, the Lord will faithfully confront the individual. Once the person is confronted and shown that he is in error, he can either accept or reject the correction.

In this particular verse, the people Peter is talking about are those in visible positions of leadership who have received correction from the Lord. They relate to Jesus not just as Lord (*Kurios*), but also as the CEO of the Church (*despotes*). He has confronted them and has said, "You're teaching divergent truth. You need to get back on track with what My Word really says." But instead of receiving the Lord's correction and repenting, they reject it and refuse to submit to Him. Furthermore, they continue to teach false doctrine, having a full understanding that what they are doing is wrong.

If these people persist down the path of error, the Bible says they will "...bring upon themselves swift destruction" (2 Peter 2:1). The word "swift" is the Greek word *tachinos*, which means *swift; sudden; quick*. And the word "destruction" is once again the Greek word *apoleia*, meaning *something that is destroyed, decayed, rotten, ruined, or devastated*. In the same way that these false teachers have planted rotten, ruinous teaching in the lives of people, they will quickly reap decay and devastation in their own lives. The sad thing is, they could have avoided it had they listened to the Lord and received His correction. Any person who submits to the Lord's correction will be forgiven and keep his position. But these particular leaders Peter is pointing out have denied the Lord, and in turn, He released them to experience the consequences of their actions.

STUDY QUESTIONS

Study to shew thyself approved unto God, a workman that needeth not to be ashamed, rightly dividing the word of truth.
— 2 Timothy 2:15

In this lesson, we learned that the false teachers Peter talked about were once authentic believers who swallowed erroneous teaching somewhere along the way. This alerts us to the fact that *anyone* can fall prey to false doctrine. To keep you on the path of truth and righteousness, you can count on the Holy Spirit to bring correction in your life. Carefully read Hebrews 12:6-13.

1. The Lord's discipline in your life is clear evidence of what?
2. If your Heavenly Father didn't discipline you, what would it mean?
3. Ultimately, what is God's purpose in correcting you? What positive effects can you expect when you cooperate with Him and receive His discipline? (Also *consider* Proverbs 15:5; John 15:2; James 1:12.)

PRACTICAL APPLICATION

> But be ye doers of the word, and not hearers only,
> deceiving your own selves.
> —James 1:22

The word "denying" in Second Peter 2:1 is the Greek word *arneomai*, which means *to knowingly deny; to knowingly disown; to knowingly reject; to knowingly refuse; or to knowingly renounce.* It depicts *something done with one's full consent and understanding of what he or she is doing.* The use of this word actually reveals the faithfulness of God to His people. If a person is in error, the Lord will faithfully confront him.

1. Has the Holy Spirit been trying to correct an area of your life where you have gotten off course? If so, what has He spoken to you?

2. Have you accepted His correction? If so, what specific steps have you taken to adjust your life and walk in obedience?

3. If you have rejected His correction, how does this lesson help you see the Lord's rebuke in a different light and motivate you to repent?

LESSON 4

TOPIC

Contending for the Faith in the Last Days

SCRIPTURES

1. **1 Timothy 4:1** — Now the Spirit speaketh expressly, that in the latter times some shall depart from the faith, giving heed to seducing spirits and doctrines of demons.

2. **Jude 3** — Beloved, when I gave all diligence to write unto you of the common salvation, it was needful for me to write you, and exhort you that ye should earnestly contend for the faith which was once delivered unto the saints.

GREEK WORDS

1. "needful" — ἀνάγκη (*anagke*): an urgent necessity

2. "exhort" — παρακαλέω (*parakaleo*): to urge, beseech, beg, or even encourage; often used by military leaders or commanding officers before they sent their troops into battle

3. "earnestly contend" — ἐπαγωνίζομαι (*epagonidzomai*): a compound of ἐπί (*epi*) and ἀγωνίζομαι (*agonidzomai*); ἐπί (*epi*) means for or over; ἀγωνίζομαι (*agonidzomai*) denotes an intense struggle, and it is where we derive the word "agony"; pictures two wrestlers who agonize to defeat the other in a wrestling match; both wrestlers work to gain the advantage and to hurl their opponent to the ground, exerting every ounce of their strength to win a physical contest; depicts those who are fighting with all their might to win a match of some type; to fight over an issue or to fight for a truth; pictures people who are wrestling between issues of truth and deception

4. "the faith" — πίστεως (*pisteos*): refers to doctrine or to the long-held, time-tested teachings of Scripture

5. "once" — ἅπαξ (*hapax*): once for all; idea of completion, finality, or something so complete that it needs nothing more to be added to it

6. "delivered" — παραδίδωμι (*paradidomi*): to deliver over to someone; to entrust to someone for safekeeping; to hand something down from one generation to the next, similar to traditions that are passed from one generation to the next in a family

SYNOPSIS

In the very heart of the city of Ephesus was Domitian Square, and in this square, there was a very large, magnificent fountain. Over the years, this highly ornamental monument has had several names, but most often it has been called the Domitian Fountain because of its location in the square next to the Temple of Domitian. Indeed, Emperor Domitian cultivated and established much opulence in the city of Ephesus. Yet he was a demented leader who did everything in his power to eradicate the Christian faith — including the imprisonment of the apostle John on the Isle of Patmos.

In spite of Domitian's relentless opposition, the church of Ephesus became a thriving, prospering conduit of God's mighty power. And yet the apostle Paul prophesied that at the very end of the age, there would be an invasion of seducing spirits and doctrines of demons that would begin to lead believers away from the time-tested truth of Scripture (*see* 1 Timothy 4:1). Jesus also spoke of this worldwide deception and said it would be the foremost sign that preceded His coming (*see* Matthew 24:4). Moreover, Peter prophesied that there would be false teachers who would bring damnable heresies into the Church in the last days, even denying the Lord who redeemed them (*see* 2 Peter 2:1). Again and again and again, the Holy Spirit reiterated a warning of great deception that would occur in the end times. He sounds this alarm not to *scare* us, but to *prepare* us for what's ahead.

The emphasis of this lesson:
Jude, the half-brother of Jesus, also spoke of ungodly men sneaking into the Church.

A Review of Paul's Warning to Timothy

Even before the New Testament Scriptures were done being written, a spiritual attack was being waged against the Gospel. Looking back at our foundational verse in First Timothy 4:1, Paul wrote, "Now the Spirit speaketh expressly, that in the latter times some shall depart from the faith, giving heed to seducing spirits and doctrines of demons."

We've seen that the phrase "speaketh expressly" is the Greek word *rhetos*, which describes *something emphatic, certain, and sure*. The Holy Spirit used the strongest and clearest language here to let us know that what He was about to say was definitely going to take place in the "latter times" and nothing would stop it.

The word "latter" is the Greek word *husteros*, which describes *the ultimate end or the very last of something*. And the word "times" in Greek is the word *kairos*, which means *a season*. Thus the Holy Spirit was pointing to the very end of the last season of time on earth, warning us of what would come.

He declared that during the last of the last days, "some shall depart from the faith." We learned that the word "depart" is the Greek word *aphistemi*, which means *to stand apart from; to distance one's self from; to step away from; to withdraw from; or to shrink away from*. This word depicts *a very slow, subtle move away from one position to another position*. It this case, it is a gradual, almost imperceptible departure from "the faith," which is the sound teaching of Scripture.

The reason for this departure is the result of people "…giving heed to seducing spirits and doctrines of devils." The phrase "giving heed" is the Greek word *prosecho*. It is a compound of two Greek words: the word *pros*, which means *to lean toward*, and the word *echo*, which means *to hold or to embrace*. When the words *pros* and *echo* are joined to form the word *prosecho*, it pictures *a person who has believed and held on to one thing for a very long time now leaning in a new direction believing something else.*

Thankfully, the Lord said that only *some* would depart from the faith — not everyone. The truth is, at the same time that some are departing, there will also be a great outpouring of the Holy Spirit birthing new believers into God's Kingdom. Thus the last days will simultaneously be the worst of times and the best of times. This description is a clear picture of what we are experiencing right now.

Jude Urgently Sounded the Alarm

This issue of deception, seducing spirits, and a departure from the faith was so important that the Holy Spirit addressed it through Jesus, the apostle Paul, the apostle Peter, and by Jude the half-brother of Jesus. It's interesting to note that it was Peter's letter, which included the warning about the false teachers spreading damnable heresies, that greatly stirred Jude's spirit and caused him to address the same issue.

Initially, Jude had planned to write about salvation, but his plan was interrupted by the news that error-filled teachings were trying to infiltrate the Church. In verse 3 of his epistle, He said, "Beloved, when I gave all diligence to write unto you of the common salvation, it was needful for me to write you, and exhort you that ye should earnestly contend for the faith which was once delivered unto the saints."

The word "needful" in this verse is the Greek word *anagke*, and it describes *an urgent necessity.* The use of this word was the equivalent of Jude's saying, "This is something I just have to do and do immediately. After hearing about the dreadful and critical things happening in the Church, I am compelled to respond right now."

Jude said his purpose in writing was to "exhort" the believers. The word "exhort" is the Greek word *parakaleo*, which means *to urge, beseech, beg, or even encourage.* This was a practice *often used by military leaders or commanding officers before they sent their troops into battle.* The commanders would summon their soldiers and explain to them the kind of battle they were about to face. They didn't deny the fact that a battle was imminent, nor did they hope it would just go away.

On the contrary, the commanders would rally their troops together and say things like, "Friends, there's a real fight in front of us, and it's going to be difficult. There may even be bloodshed." The leaders would urge, beg, and plead with their soldiers to stand tall, throw back their shoulders, look the enemy straight in the face, and march forward into the fray unflinchingly.

That is the idea Jude had when he wrote his letter to the believers in his day and in our day. "Error is trying to enter the Church, and it is our responsibility as God's people to drive the devil's deception out of our territory."

Believers Are To 'Earnestly Contend' for the Faith

Next, Jude urged us to "…earnestly contend for the faith…." The words "earnestly contend" are from the Greek word *epagonidzomai*, which is a compound of the words *epi* and *agonidzomai*. The word *epi* means *for or over*; the word *agonidzomai* denotes *an intense struggle*. It is where we derive the word "agony." This word pictures *two wrestlers who agonize to defeat the other in a wrestling match*. Both wrestlers work to gain the advantage and to hurl their opponent to the ground, exerting *every ounce of their strength to win a physical contest*. The word *epagonidzomai* can also depict *those who are fighting with all their might to win a match of some type*. Furthermore, it can mean *to fight over an issue or to fight for a truth*. It pictures *people who are wrestling between issues of truth and deception*.

Taking into account the meaning of this word, Jude used his letter to ready all his readers to prepare themselves to march into the battle. They were not to take the fight lightly, but to give it all they had. It would likely be an agonizing struggle against the enemy. Specifically, it was a fight for "the faith."

Just as we saw in First Timothy 4:1, the Greek construction here shows that the word "faith" is accompanied by a definite article. This means "the faith" doesn't refer to faith for miracles or faith for supernatural signs and wonders. When Jude said "the faith," he used the Greek word *pisteos* and was referring specifically to *doctrine, or to the long-held, time-tested teachings of Scripture*.

False teachers were wrestling with people over the truth. In fact they were trying to wrestle the truth out of the hands of believers and replace it with a divergent, modified version. They were attempting to smuggle error into the Church, encouraging people to embrace compromise. Knowing this, Jude was urging believers to get in the fight and wrestle their opponents to the ground, so to speak, not letting them steal away the truth. The Holy Spirit was calling on his readers — and He's calling upon us in our day — to take a stance for truth and to refuse to budge from what is right.

Scripture Needs No Modifications

Jude stated that the faith "...was once delivered unto the saints." The word "once" is the Greek word *hapax*, which means *once for all*. It carries the idea of *completion, finality*, or *something so complete that it needs nothing more to be added to it*. The word *hapax* — translated here as "once" — helps us understand what these errant teachers were doing. They were altering, amending, and attempting to make improvements to the truth that had "once for all" been delivered. They didn't like the truth because it inconvenienced their lives. Therefore, they were trying to create a new version of the truth — one that was more palatable for pagans and unbelievers. They wanted something that was more inclusive in which everyone could participate.

When Jude said that the faith was "once delivered unto the saints," he was saying, "It needs no amendments, no alterations, and no deletions. It is complete, final, and needs nothing more added to it." Again, Jude was talking about the Word of God when he said this.

We don't need to change the truth of Scripture — we need to let the truth change *us*. We need to study it and make sure we are in the process of fully understanding it. God wants us to live and speak the truth in such a way that it changes our culture.

Are you beginning to see why the devil hates the Bible so intensely? Can you see why he works so diligently to discredit its value and to get people to believe it is an outdated book of fables? Satan knows that when the truth of Scripture is declared, embraced, and believed, it releases dynamic power that drives out darkness.

Our Job Is To Pass on Pure Truth
to the Next Generation

Jude said that the faith was "once delivered unto the saints." The word "delivered" here is the Greek word *paradidomi*, which means *to deliver over to someone; to entrust to someone for safekeeping; to hand something down from one generation to the next, similar to traditions that are passed from one generation to the next in a family.*

Traditions can easily be lost. If they're not lost altogether, they can be altered from one generation to the next — unless someone cares enough to preserve them. Jude said the Word was "delivered" to us for safekeeping.

In order to keep a tradition alive, it has to be passed on to the next generation. If you make a decision to celebrate your traditions and pass them on to your children, they will live. The same is true for the truth of Scripture. God's Word was passed on to you, and you need to pass it on to others. We have been entrusted by God with the responsibility to take the Word that is complete and needs no additions or deletions — and to declare it in its purest form.

STUDY QUESTIONS

> **Study to shew thyself approved unto God, a workman that needeth not to be ashamed, rightly dividing the word of truth.**
> **— 2 Timothy 2:15**

Jude said that the faith — the time-tested teachings of Scripture — were "…was once delivered unto the saints." The word "once" is the Greek word *hapax*, which means *once for all*. It carries *the idea of completion, finality,* or *something so complete that it needs nothing more to be added to it.*

1. Again and again, the Holy Spirit reassures us about a characteristic of God's Word. What is that characteristic? (*See* Psalm 12:6; 18:30; Proverbs 30:5.)

2. What urgent warning regarding Scripture is repeated in Deuteronomy 4:2; Proverbs 30:6, and Revelation 22:19?

3. According to these verses, what are the consequences of disobeying this command?

PRACTICAL APPLICATION

> But be ye doers of the word, and not hearers only,
> deceiving your own selves.
> —James 1:22

1. The Church was birthed in the First Century, and from its inception, people have attempted to twist and change the truth to fit their desires, their agenda, and their lifestyle. Take a moment to pray, "Holy Spirit, am I doing this anywhere in my own life? If so, please show me that I might repent and adjust my life to Your truth, in Jesus' Name."

2. God has called you to help pass on the truth of God's Word to the next generation in its purest form. Stop and think: *In what specific ways am I helping to pass on the faith to my children, grandchildren, and those younger than me over whom I have a degree of influence?*

3. After hearing this lesson on "Contending for the Faith in the Last Days," what action steps do you sense the Holy Spirit is prompting you to take?

LESSON 5

TOPIC

How To Pray for Leaders Who Are in Error

SCRIPTURES

1. **1 Timothy 4:1** — Now the Spirit speaketh expressly, that in the latter times some shall depart from the faith, giving heed to seducing spirits and doctrines of demons.

2. **Jude 22-23** — And of some have compassion, making a difference: and others save with fear, pulling them out of the fire; hating even the garment spotted by the flesh.

GREEK WORDS

1. "compassion" — ἐλεέω (*eleeo*): depicts the deep-seated and unsettling emotions a person feels when he has seen or heard something terribly sad or upsetting

2. "making a difference" — διακρίνω (*diakrino*): to distinguish or judge; pictures an individual who has lost his ability to separate right from wrong; can depict those unable to tell the difference between the truth and a lie

3. "pulling" — ἁρπάζω (*harpadzo*): the picture of laying hold of and snatching someone out of a dangerous situation

SYNOPSIS

The city of Ephesus was home to the largest and most vibrant church on the continent of Asia. God moved mightily among the believers there, performing many great signs and wonders. The Church of Ephesus was such a role model to other churches that it became a training ground for people to be launched out into ministry. After the apostle Paul established this church and was forced to move on due to persecution, he appointed Timothy to be the pastor over the congregation.

For many years, Timothy faithfully served the Body of Christ in Ephesus. Then at the age of 80, history tells us that he was marched out into the street and martyred for his faith. In all his years of ministry, Timothy never deviated from the truth of Scripture that was handed down to him by his grandmother Lois, his mother Eunice, and his mentor Paul. His leadership was solid, unlike the false teachers that Paul and Peter prophesied would surface in the Last Days.

The emphasis of this lesson:

In these last days, there will be leaders who are led astray by seducing spirits and doctrines of demons. God has called you to receive His compassion and pray fervently for them to come to their senses and to repent.

Speaking through the apostle Paul, the Holy Spirit said, "Now the Spirit speaketh expressly, that in the latter times some shall depart from the faith, giving heed to seducing spirits and doctrines of demons" (1Timothy 4:1). This is our anchor verse for this series, and here is a quick review of some of the key words and their meanings that we have learned:

"Speaketh expressly" is the Greek word *rhetos*, and it means *emphatically or definitely*. It describes *something that will most assuredly come to pass*. In this case, the Holy Spirit was emphatically declaring that "in the latter times some shall depart from the faith."

"Latter" is the Greek word *husteros*, and it describes *the very end of something; nothing is left in the season*. In the context of this verse, the word *husteros* is connected with the word "times," which is the Greek word describing *a season*. The Holy Spirit is pointing to the very end of the age when there is virtually no more time remaining, telling us what is going to happen then.

"Some shall depart from the faith." The word "depart" is the Greek word *aphestemi*, and it describes *a very slow, gradual, step-by-step move away from one position in order to move toward a new position*. This departure is so subtle and imperceptible that those who are in the transition may not even realize they're doing it. The withdrawal that is taking place is from "the faith."

"The faith" in Greek includes the definite article, so it is not just any type of faith. It is specifically "the faith," which indicates *the sound teaching of Scripture*. This is what *some* — not everyone — will depart from in the last of the last days.

"Giving heed to seducing spirits and doctrines of demons." The phrase "giving heed" is the Greek word *prosecho*, which is a compound of two words: the word *pros*, which means *to lean forward*, and the word *echo*, which means *to embrace*. When these two words are combined to form the word *prosecho*, it describes *someone that is leaning forward in a new direction to embrace something*. In this case, he or she is leaning away from the sound teaching of Scripture and leaning toward a divergent, modified version of the truth.

The force behind this departure from the faith is seducing spirits and doctrines of devils. Paul, Peter, Jesus, and Jude all prophesied of the dark deception that would come at the very end of the age, and they identified Satan and his minions as the source behind it. Although culture, trends, and society are constantly changing, God's Word never changes. The truth is always the truth — regardless of people's opinions or any other contributing factor.

God has called us to "earnestly contend for the faith…" (Jude 3). In the Greek, the phrase "earnestly contend" is the word *epagonidzomai*, which means *to really wrestle* over, *to fight over*. In the context of this verse, God wants us to fight for "the faith," which is the same Greek word used in First Timothy 4:1 that signifies *the unadulterated truth of Scripture*. As we wrestle against the forces of evil, God wants us to hold tightly to His Word and not let anyone wrestle it out of our hands.

What Can You Do If Someone You Know Has Wandered From the Faith?

Do you know someone who has been led astray by seducing spirits and doctrines of demons? Maybe it is a spiritual leader who has poured into your life for many years, helping to shape and mold you into the child of God you are today. Maybe it is your spouse, a child, a sibling, or a treasured friend who once walked intimately close with the Lord, but somehow, somewhere along the way began to embrace ideas that are blatantly against Scripture. When you hear of the philosophies and doctrines this person is now teaching and endorsing, you can hardly believe it.

How should you respond? Getting angry and staying offended with people in this condition will not shake them from their delusion. Verbally assaulting them to their face or cutting them down in the hearing of others won't help either. Are you simply left to wring your hands and worry about their wellbeing? Thankfully, not. God gives us clear direction on how we should respond in such situations, and He speaks to us through Jude.

God Calls Us To Have Compassion

After Jude urged believers — both then and now — to contend for the faith (*see* v. 3), he explained how we are to respond to people who have wandered from the truth of Scripture. In verses 22 and 23, he said, "And of some have compassion, making a difference: and others save with fear, pulling them out of the fire; hating even the garment spotted by the flesh."

The word "compassion" in verse 22 is the Greek word *eleao*, and it depicts *the deep-seated and unsettling emotions a person feels when he has seen or heard something terribly sad or upsetting*. It is the picture of a person who is not just profoundly disturbed, but also moved to do something about the situation. It is a godly-infused compassion that moves us to action.

It is important to note that the word "compassion" here is not just pity. Pity has little to no value. True "compassion" — the Greek word *eleao* — actually describes the emotions you might feel when you see someone in a deplorable of hopeless situation.

- Like the emotions you feel when you see an emaciated person dying of terminal cancer.
- Like the emotions you feel when you encounter a family living in destitute conditions.
- Like the emotions you feel when you see a starving child whose stomach is bloated from malnutrition.

Normally, if you see someone in such conditions, you don't just shake your head in disbelief or voice how pitiful their situation is. Instead, *you are moved to take action*. You give to an organization that you know is actively caring for the sick, helping the homeless, or feeding the hungry. If the situation permits, you may even personally get involved.

By using this word *eleao*, translated here as "compassion," Jude is telling us that the spiritual condition of wayward believers — and errant spiritual leaders — is just as serious as the plight of a starving child, a dying man or woman, or a destitute family. It is this kind of compassion God wants to cultivate in you that will move you to action on behalf of a compromised leader.

Prayer Is the Most Important Action You Can Take

Please realize that being trapped in error is a very serious issue. When you see or hear of a leader who has wandered away from the time-tested truth of Scripture, let your concerns move you *to pray*. As you begin to pray for God to have mercy on them and open their eyes to truth, the Holy Spirit will begin to soften your heart and release a divine flow of His compassion in your heart.

The Bible says in James 5:16, "…The effectual fervent prayer of a righteous man availeth much." This same verse in the *Amplified Bible* says, "…The earnest (heartfelt, continued) prayer of a righteous man makes tremendous power available [dynamic in its working]." This promise lets us know that when you sincerely lift a person up in prayer to God, you can be confident that He will hear you and your prayer will release His power in their life and in yours.

Compassion is a mighty force that releases astonishing amounts of spiritual power. The flow of God's power has the ability to break chains that bind people's minds and hearts. This is why Jude urged us, "And of some have compassion...."

You Can Make a Difference

When you operate in the divine compassion of God, the Bible says you can be confident that you're "making a difference." The Greek word for "making a difference" is *diakrino*, and it describes *an individual who has lost his ability to separate right from wrong*. It can also depict *those unable to tell the difference between the truth and a lie*.

Sometimes people have been so inundated with lies and false images that it begins to affect the way they think. Their hearts often become calloused and their minds reprobate. This is a picture of what the word *diakrino* means. It describes believers or spiritual leaders who have gone astray — developing a chronic instability in what they believe. Ultimately they begin to doubt God's Word altogether — often even questioning the most basic fundamentals of scriptural truth.

By using the word *diakrino* — translated here as "making a difference" — Jude tells us that deceived individuals are unable to reach accurate spiritual conclusions. Instead of standing up for the truth, they water it down and even apologize for what the Bible says. A result, they embrace and promote what they once deemed to be spiritual error or to be morally wrong.

How does one sink to such a level? Again, it goes back to "seducing spirits" that lured them off track little by little over a period of time. Somewhere along the way, they let go of the truth that was once precious and dear and they began to open their mind and heart to new systems of thought.

God's Word says you can make a difference in the lives of people in this (*diakrino*) condition. The key is prayer and cultivating a heart of compassion.

You Can Pull People Out of the Fire

Jude continues in verse 23, urging us to "…save with fear, pulling them out of the fire; hating even the garment spotted by the flesh." The word "pulling" is the Greek word *harpadzo*, which is the picture of *laying hold of and snatching someone out of a dangerous situation*. Through prayer — empowered by divine compassion — we must lay hold of people in spiritually dangerous predicaments and snatch them from destruction.

Lot, Abraham's nephew, is a perfect example. He had shadowed his uncle Abraham for many years after they left the city of Haran and traveled throughout Canaan. When Abraham built an altar and worshipped the Lord, Lot was there helping and participating. When Abraham went down to Egypt because of the severe famine in the land, Lot witnessed the hand of God's protection and blessing. Lot knew what it meant to walk in faith and fellowship with God, but he veered off course.

After he pitched his tent toward Sodom, Lot eventually moved into the city and became an elected official. His thinking became so twisted by the seducing spirits he had been listening to that he called the perverted, homosexual men of Sodom his "brethren" (*see* Genesis 19:7). Eventually, the cry of Sodom's sin reached the ears of God in Heaven, and He came down to judge the city. Lot was totally oblivious to the sudden destruction that was just around the corner for him and his family, which demonstrates how wayward believers often don't realize the seriousness of their condition.

Abraham, on the other hand, walked in fellowship with the Lord daily and learned of God's impending judgment. Immediately, he began to intercede for Lot and his family, and Abraham — through his prayers — snatched Lot out of the fire of destruction. Had Abraham not prayed for Lot, he would have experienced the negative consequences of his choices.

When people are lured off track, we must pray and seek the guidance of the Holy Spirit. He will show us how to pray so they can be delivered from the judgment they are about to bring upon themselves. As you draw near to the Lord in prayer, a divine stream of compassion will begin to flow, and your effectual, fervent prayer will make tremendous power available. Like Abraham, your prayers will pull (*harpadzo*) that person out of the fire.

Putting the meanings of all these words together, here is the *Renner Interpretive Version (RIV)* for Jude 22 and 23:

> **You must have a compassionate attitude toward those so spiritually calloused that they no longer know the difference between right and wrong. The truth is, these unstable people are living right on the brink of disaster and are in real spiritual jeopardy. Their plight is so grave that it requires you put into action an immediate rescue plan to snatch them from the fires of destruction....**

The Holy Spirit prophesied that there would be an increased activity of seducing spirits and doctrines of demons at the end of this age. That long-prophesied time has arrived. We are living in the midst of mind-boggling deception. If you know of a leader, a family member, or a friend who has veered from the truth of Scripture and you're shocked by what that person is doing and endorsing, don't stay in that state of shock. Let your concern drive you to prayer that will release a divine stream of compassion in your heart. Your prayers can reach into the fire and pull that wayward person from the flames just in the nick of time.

STUDY QUESTIONS

> **Study to shew thyself approved unto God, a workman that needeth not to be ashamed, rightly dividing the word of truth.**
> **— 2 Timothy 2:15**

The action that will reach into the fires of destruction and snatch people from the flames before they're destroyed is your *prayers*. Divine compassion moves you to pray, and your prayers release divine compassion. James 5:16 says, "...The effectual fervent prayer of a righteous man availeth much."

1. If you're thinking, *I'm not righteous. There are still areas in my life where I stumble and fall.* Take time to meditate on the truth of Second Corinthians 5:21 and declare it aloud over your life.

2. If you're wondering, *I'm not a pastor or a prophet. Can my prayers really make a difference?* Read James 5:13-20. What do you and Elijah have in common? How is Jude 22 and 23 similar to James 5:19 and 20? What else is the Holy Spirit showing you in these verses?

PRACTICAL APPLICATION

But be ye doers of the word, and not hearers only,
deceiving your own selves.
—James 1:22

1. Look back over your life. Have *you* ever been in error? Have you ever been the recipient of someone else's prayers that exposed the enemy's lies and opened your eyes to the truth? If so, briefly describe the situation and tell how those prayers made a difference in your life.

2. Who do you know who has been led astray by seducing spirits and doctrines of demons? It is your spouse, a child, a sibling, or a treasured friend? What is it about them and their situation that grieves your heart so deeply?

3. *Prayer* for this person is the most important and powerful action you can take. Instead of getting mad or remaining sad, let your concerns move you to pray. Take time right now to sincerely and earnestly bring before the Lord this person who is in trouble.

LESSON 6

TOPIC

Timothy's Situation With Erring Leaders

SCRIPTURES

1. **1 Timothy 4:1** — Now the Spirit speaketh expressly, that in the latter times some shall depart from the faith, giving heed to seducing spirits and doctrines of demons.

2. **1 Timothy 1:3** — As I besought thee to abide still at Ephesus that thou mightest charge some that they teach no other doctrine.

3. **2 Peter 2:1** — But there were false prophets among the people, even as there shall be false teachers among you, who privily shall bring in damnable heresies, even denying the Lord that bought them, and bring upon themselves swift destruction.

GREEK WORDS

1. "besought" — **παρακαλέω** (*parakaleo*): to urge, beseech, beg, or even encourage; often used by military leaders or commanding officers before they sent their troops into battle

2. "mightest charge" — **παραγγέλλω** (*parangello*): to order, charge, or give a command; to strictly charge; it is a direct command

3. "some" — **τισιν** (*tisin*): a certain some; a notable some; certain ones

4. "other doctrine" — **ἐτεροδιδασκαλέω** (*heterodidaskaleo*): a compound of **ἕτερος** (*heteros*) and **διδάσκαλος** (*didaskalos*); the word **ἕτερος** (*heteros*) points to something of a different kind, and the word **διδάσκαλος** (*didaskalos*) depicts doctrine or teaching; compounded, **ἐτεροδιδασκαλέω** (*heterodidaskaleo*) means to teach another doctrine; pictures a doctrine of a different kind or a teaching of a different sort

5. "privily shall bring in" — **παρεισάγω** (*pareisago*): a compound of three Greek words: **παρά** (*para*), which means alongside; **εἰς** (*eis*), which means into; and **ἄγω** (*ago*), which means to lead; the word **παρά** (*para*) in this context indicates that the false teachers Peter referenced will walk alongside other believers; **εἰς** (*eis*) means they will bring their false doctrines right into the church; and **ἄγω** (*ago*) suggests that these individuals will hold positions of leadership in the church; when compounded, as in Second Peter 2:1, denotes a smuggler attempting to covertly transport illegal contraband across a border while using a disguise or stealth to conceal his activities

SYNOPSIS

The city of Ephesus has an extremely rich history. People from all parts of the globe have been drawn there for thousands of years. It continues to be the most visited archaeological site in the world. Ephesus was home to the largest, most influential church on the continent of Asia. It was founded during the middle of the First Century by the concerted efforts of the apostle Paul and his co-laborers Aquila and Priscilla. When it came time for Paul to leave, he installed Timothy as the pastor of the Ephesian church. As time progressed, some of the church leaders began to drift away from the foundation of Scripture. When Paul heard what was happening, he wrote to Timothy and urged him to deal with the issue of erring leaders.

The emphasis of this lesson:

In a world where erring leaders are modifying truth to accommodate ungodly lifestyles, we must hold tightly to the time-tested truth of Scripture and respectfully correct those who are in error.

The Battle for Truth Continues To Rage

Writing under the unction of the Holy Spirit, the apostle Paul prophesied what was going to happen in the world and in the Church at the very end of the age. In First Timothy 4:1, Paul wrote, "Now the Spirit speaketh expressly, that in the latter times some shall depart from the faith, giving heed to seducing spirits and doctrines of devils."

The phrase "speaketh expressly" in this verse is the Greek word *rhetos*, and it describes *something that is absolutely, without question, going to take place.* There is no *might* or *maybe* about it. This part of the verse could be translated, "Now the Spirit speaks in the strongest and clearest language possible that something is definitely coming...."

When is coming? The Spirit said, "...In the latter times...." The word "latter" is the Greek word *husteros*, and it describes *the ultimate end of something when nothing is left over.* And the word "times" is the Greek word *kairos*, which means *a season.* Thus, when we arrive at the very outer rim of the end of the age, just before everything is wrapped up, something very strange is going to take place in the Church worldwide.

The Bible says, "Some shall depart from the faith." The good news is that not everyone will depart from the faith, but according to the Greek used here, it will be *a noticeable number of people.* The departure is from "the faith." By including the definite article here, we know "the faith" is not faith for signs and wonders or faith for miracles and healing. It is "the faith," which means *the hardcore teachings of Scripture.* This is what some people in the Church will "depart" from in latter times.

To be clear, *departing* is not the same as *rejecting.* The Holy Spirit doesn't say that people will *reject* the teaching of Scripture. He says they will "depart" from it. The word "depart" is the Greek word *aphistemi*, which describes *a step-by-step, inch-by-inch, day-by-day moving away from the teaching of the Bible.* It is a subtle, gradual, almost imperceptible distancing of oneself from the timeless truths of God's Word. In many cases, those people aren't even aware that they are departing.

This departure from Scripture, which will take place at the very end of the age had already begun during the First Century. In fact, a battle was immediately underway, at the Church's inception, which is what prompted Paul to write and warn Timothy.

Paul Begged Timothy To Deal With the False Teachers

As previously noted, Paul appointed Timothy to be the pastor of the Church of Ephesus when he was forced to move to another region due to persecution. History records that Luke played a role in the development of the church, and Mary, the mother of Jesus, began attending the church of Ephesus when the apostle John was the presiding elder over the fellowship. Indeed, it was a thriving place, marked by God's miracles and the rich teaching of His Word.

Yet in spite of Ephesus' greatness, the church there came to a place where a number of its leaders began to gradually distance themselves from the foundational teachings of Scripture. When Paul received word of the departure that was taking place, he wrote to Timothy and brought it to his attention. In First Timothy 1:3, he said, "As I besought thee to abide still at Ephesus that thou mightest charge some that they teach no other doctrine."

First, notice the word "besought." It is the Greek word *parakaleo*, which means *to urge, beseech, beg, or encourage*. This word was often used by military leaders or commanding officers before they sent their troops into battle. Essentially, Paul *begged* and *pleaded* with Timothy to bring correction to those who were beginning to stray from the faith. It was Timothy's responsibility as the pastor to deal with it.

Next, Paul said, "…That thou mightiest charge some that they teach no other doctrine." The word "charge" here is the Greek word *parangello*, and it means *to order, charge, or give a command; to strictly charge*. And the word "some" is the Greek word *tisin*, which describes *a certain some; a notable some; certain ones*. Paul didn't say *every* leader in Ephesus had given in to the influence of seducing spirits and doctrines of demons. Only *some* had. The same is true regarding leaders in the last days. Not everyone will be led astray. Many leaders will hold tightly to the truth and refuse to budge.

They Were Teaching 'Doctrine of a Different Kind'

Even so, Paul told Timothy to give a strict, direct command to the notable number of people who were beginning to depart from Scripture "...that they teach no other doctrine." The phrase "other doctrine" is the Greek word *heterodidaskaleo*. It is a compound of the word *heteros*, which points to *something different or of a different kind*, and the word *didaskalos*, which depicts *doctrine or teaching*. When these two words are compounded to form the word *heterodidaskaleo*, it means *to teach another doctrine*, and it pictures *a doctrine of a different kind* or *a teaching of a different sort*.

Paul used this word to tell us unquestionably that some notable individuals were disseminating *doctrines* and *teaching of a different kind*. As false teachers always do, they were mingling truth and error together, and it sounded very polished and sophisticated. But Paul said the teaching (*didaskalos*) was *heteros* — of a different kind.

This same word — *heterodidaskaleo* — was used by Paul in Galatians 1:6 and 7. He said, "I marvel that ye are so soon removed from him that called you into the grace of Christ unto another gospel: which is not another; but there be some that trouble you, and would pervert the gospel of Christ."

In effect, the same thing that was happening in Ephesus was occurring among the Galatians. The errant teachers were not bringing blatant false doctrine. Instead, they were mingling error with the truth. Although there were elements of the Gospel being presented, it was mixed with error, and as a result, the Galatians were troubled or confused by what they were hearing.

Error Was Cleverly Mingled With Truth

Like Paul, the apostle Peter prophesied about the emergence of errant teachers as well. He said, "But there were false prophets among the people, even as there shall be false teachers among you, who privily shall bring in damnable heresies, even denying the Lord that bought them, and bring upon themselves swift destruction."

In one of our previous lessons, we learned the meaning of the phrase "privily shall bring in." It is the Greek word *pareisago*, which is a compound of three words: *para*, which means *alongside*; *eis*, which means *into*; and *ago*, which means *to lead*. The word *para* in this context indicates that the false teachers Peter referenced will walk *alongside* other believers. The word *eis* means they will bring their false doctrines right *into* the church. And the word *ago* suggests that these individuals will hold positions of *leadership* in the church. When these three words are compounded to form *pareisago*, as in Second Peter 2:1, it denotes *a smuggler attempting to covertly transport illegal contraband across a border while using a disguise or stealth to conceal his activities.*

Just as with other false teachers, these errant leaders knew they couldn't just teach blatant error, so they mixed it with truth to make it less recognizable. This was especially troublesome for new, immature believers. Paul, Peter, and Jude all prophesied that this would happen at the very end of the age, and it was already occurring in the First Century.

Gnostics Were Masterful at Mixing Error With Truth — and the Same Errors Are Re-Emerging

Timothy also dealt with people who were mixing error with truth. At the time he assumed his pastoral role in Ephesus, a group of leaders was emerging who later became known as Gnostics. They claimed to be enlightened and have supreme revelation. The term "Gnostics" is derived from the Greek word *gnosis*, which means *knowledge*. Gnosticism was *a commingling of Christian beliefs with pagan ideas.* Once mixed together, another "gospel" was created — one that was more compatible with the pagan world.

There were many Gnostic errors taught in the First Century, and they were believed by some in the Church. The doctrines of the Gnostics are the same errors that false teachers are trying to propagate now, at the end of the age. Remember, the source of all lies is Satan — the father of lies. He is using the same strategy today that he used 2,000 years ago. Here is a list of six of the major Gnostic errors that Timothy had to refute.

Error #1: The Gnostics claimed Old Testament Scriptures were inferior and were based on old, outdated, and antiquated ideas. Thus, Christians needed to disconnect themselves from the teachings of the Old Testament.

As strange as it may seem, some leaders today are also claiming that the Old Testament has no relevance for New Testament believers. Some leaders go so far as to say that Christians must "unhitch" from the writings of the Old Testament. This notion is preposterous. Any good student of the Bible knows that much of the Old Testament is reflected in the New Testament, and Jesus quoted from the Old Testament all the time. To say it is irrelevant is ludicrous.

Error #2: Gnostics proposed the idea that the wrath of the Old Testament God wasn't to be taken seriously by New Testament believers. They contended that all forms of present or future judgment were dismissed. Gnostics claimed that the concept of God's wrath was an imaginary doctrine based on religious thinking that should be discounted as unfitting for a loving God.

Does that sound familiar? Some teachers today skillfully assert that the idea of God's wrath is antiquated and outdated. They claim that because God's wrath was poured out on Christ, there is no more divine wrath to release in a future judgment. But anyone educated in theology understands the fallacy of this teaching.

Error #3: Gnostics also held to a doctrine that the flesh — indeed, all physical matter — was evil and fading. Only the spirit held significance. So once a person's spirit was born again, it really didn't matter whether he sinned with the flesh. Thus, no one needed to confess any sin after he came to Christ.

This Gnostic doctrine led people to believe sin was inconsequential. It gave the impression that there was no need for repentance for any wrong act conducted in the flesh. Anyone educated in Church history will understand this is one of the premises of Gnosticism that is again attempting to establish a foothold in the Church in these last days.

Error #4: Gnostics were "antinomian." The word "antinomian" means *against law*, and it depicts *Gnostic aversion to the moral law of God*, which they alleged to be an inferior, Old Testament concept that had no relevance for Christians.

This is precisely what some are teaching today when they dismiss the textual authority of the Old Testament and even declare that the Ten Commandments have no relevance for a modern-day believer. When you hear this type of thinking, know it is Gnosticism trying to gain a foothold again in this end-time hour.

Error #5: Gnostics also believed that a "new" gospel was needed that would merge varying religious beliefs. They attempted to create a message that was more open-minded, less text-based, and more "inclusive" of other theological beliefs, philosophical ideas, and alternative lifestyles. Gnostics sought to create a faith that even unbelievers would consider unobjectionable and be able to participate in.

Errant teachers today are doing precisely what the Gnostics of the New Testament times were doing. They attempt to remove everything objectionable in Scripture in order to create a newly styled gospel and church environment that makes everyone accepted with no need to adapt their hearts, minds, and lives to the Scripture. This is another Gnostic practice that is being resurrected in these last days.

Error #6: Gnostics believed that God expressed Himself in various manifestations, and that Jesus was just one of them. This doctrine depreciated Christ, reducing Him to a position of "one among many" ways to Heaven.

Because of a lack of solid biblical teaching today, there are many people in the Church who do not believe Christ is the *only* way to Heaven. The belief that many roads lead to Heaven is a Gnostic concept that is resurfacing at the end of this age.

Although it is difficult to understand how early believers who actually sat under the teaching of the apostles could have been led astray by Gnostic teaching, it happened. And if it could happen then, it can certainly happen now. Today many Gnostic-like doctrines are reemerging and being perpetuated — just as the Holy Spirit forecasted in First Timothy 4:1.

And although there are many God-fearing pastors, preachers, and spiritual leaders in the Christian community today, some are repeating the errors made in early centuries of the Church. In pulpits and congregations around the world, truth is being altered to reflect the inclusive values of a changing culture. Why are so many people swallowing these recycled lies? The reason is, many people in the Church today are biblically illiterate. They are ignorant of even the most elementary tenets of the faith. The only way to avoid these same pitfalls from the past is to make a decision to dig deep into God's Word and know what it says.

STUDY QUESTIONS

Study to shew thyself approved unto God, a workman that needeth not to be ashamed, rightly dividing the word of truth.
— 2 Timothy 2:15

Carefully read the apostle Paul's concerns about believing and giving allegiance to "a different gospel" in Galatians 1:6 and 7.

1. Now read and identify his warning to believers in verses 8 and 9.

2. How do his words speak to you personally? What do you think is the significance of this warning, which is repeated twice in two consecutive verses?

3. The Holy Spirit, through the apostle John, provides a litmus test to apply to what you're hearing to help you confirm whether it is from God or not. Read First John 4:1-6 and identify this test.

PRACTICAL APPLICATION

But be ye doers of the word, and not hearers only,
deceiving your own selves.
— James 1:22

Take a few minutes to reread the six major Gnostic errors presented.

1. Of the six, which ones have you personally seen and heard trying to regain a foothold in this end-time hour? Who is teaching these deviations from truth that you need to pray for?

2. Which deception seems to be most harmful to believers? Why do you feel this is the case?

3. Which scriptures come to mind that refute these errant claims?

LESSON 7

TOPIC

The Real Problem: Lack of Bible Knowledge

SCRIPTURES

1. **1 Timothy 4:1** — Now the Spirit speaketh expressly, that in the latter times some shall depart from the faith, giving heed to seducing spirits and doctrines of demons.

2. **1 Timothy 1:3-5** — As I besought thee to abide still at Ephesus, when I went into Macedonia, that thou mightest charge some that they teach no other doctrine. Neither give heed to fables and endless genealogies, which minister questions, rather than godly edifying which is in faith: so do. Now the end of the commandment is charity out of a pure heart, and of a good conscience, and of faith unfeigned.

GREEK WORDS

1. "besought" — **παρακαλέω** (*parakaleo*): to urge, beseech, beg, or even encourage; often used by military leaders or commanding officers before they sent their troops into battle

2. "mightest charge" — **παραγγέλλω** (*parangello*): to order, charge, or give a command; to strictly charge; it is a direct command

3. "some" — **τισιν** (*tisin*): a certain some; a notable some; certain ones

4. "other doctrine" — **ἑτεροδιδασκαλέω** (*heterodidaskaleo*): a compound of ἕτερος (*heteros*) and διδάσκαλος (*didaskalos*); the word ἕτερος (heteros) points to something of a different kind, and the word διδάσκαλος (*didaskalos*) depicts doctrine or teaching; compounded, ἑτεροδιδασκαλέω (*heterodidaskaleo*) means to teach another doctrine; pictures a doctrine of a different kind or a teaching of a different sort

5. "give heed" — **προσέχω** (*prosecho*): to embrace

6. "fables" — **μῦθος** (*muthos*): a myth or fantasy; stories told in replacement of truth; in the New Testament, depicts false teaching perpetrated in place of truth

7. "endless" — **ἀπέραντος** (*aperantos*): endless; unbridled; unrestrained; unfounded; incomplete in content and thought

8. "ministers" — **παρέχω** (*parecho*): gives rise to; brings about; leads to

9. "questions" — **ἐκζητήσεις** (*ekdzeteseis*): unsolvable research; unfounded conclusions; a nonstop seeking for answers that leads to nowhere

10. "edifying" — **οἰκονομία** (*oikonomia*): an architectural term meaning to enlarge or amplify a house; depicts the careful following of an architectural plan to enlarge, increase, or amplify; improving; leaving something in an improved condition

SYNOPSIS

When people became sick in the First Century, it was primarily the result of something toxic they ate. Eating food that was not fit for consumption not only made people sick, but it often brought about their death. The same principle applies to what we consume spiritually. People who take in teaching that is spiritually imbalanced and not grounded in God's Word will become spiritually sick. In fact, it will affect every area of their life. Therefore, in order to keep our head on straight in a world gone crazy, we need to be mindful of the quality of the spiritual food we are eating.

The emphasis of this lesson:

The healthiest spiritual food we can consume is the sound doctrine of Scripture — unedited and unaltered by man. It is life-giving nourishment that produces a pure heart, a good conscience, and strong faith.

In First Timothy 4:1, Paul said, "Now the Spirit speaketh expressly, that in the latter times some shall depart from the faith, giving heed to seducing spirits and doctrines of devils." This foundational verse lets us know that at the very end of the last days — when no time remains — there will be an invasion of seducing spirits and doctrines of demons, causing some believers to drift away from solid, biblical teaching.

What will they gravitate toward? The answer is found in the word "doctrines," which is the Greek word *didaskalia*, and it describes *well-packaged, sophisticated teaching that is applicable to lifestyle.* This means the enemy is going to disseminate very seductive messages of error cleverly mingled with truth to lead people down a path to destruction.

The People Were Deceived by 'Other Doctrine'

In our last lesson, we looked at Paul's charge to Timothy, the young pastor at the Church of Ephesus. At that time there were certain distinguished and beloved leaders who later became known as Gnostics that were trying to modify and amend the Scriptures and lead believers astray just at the Holy Spirit had forecasted in First Timothy 4:1. Paul said, "As I besought thee to abide still at Ephesus, when I went into Macedonia, that thou mightest charge some that they teach no other doctrine" (1 Timothy 1:3).

We saw that the word "besought" is the Greek word *parakaleo*, which means *to urge, beseech, or beg.* By using this word, we know that Timothy did not want to deal with these false teachers. They had created such a doctrinal mess inside the church that Paul resorted to *begging* Timothy to take responsibility and deal with the issue. Timothy was to give a strict command to the notable "some" not to lead people astray with "other doctrine."

This phrase "other doctrine" is the Greek word *heterodidaskaleo*. It is a compound of the words *heteros* and *didaskalos*; the word *heteros* points to *something of a different kind*, and the word *didaskalos* depicts *doctrine or teaching*. When these two words are compounded to form the word *heterodidaskaleo*, it means *to teach another doctrine*. It pictures *a doctrine of a different kind* or *a teaching of a different sort*. This "other doctrine" was contaminated spiritual food, and it was making those who consumed it sick.

'Fables' and 'Endless Genealogies' Brought Confusion

In First Timothy 1:4, Paul went on to say, "Neither give heed to fables and endless genealogies, which minister questions, rather than godly edifying which is in faith: so do." The phrase "give heed" is the Greek word *prosecho*, which is the same word used in First Timothy 4:1 when Paul warned about "giving heed to seducing spirits and doctrines of demons." It was also used by Jesus in Matthew 24:4 when He talked about guarding ourselves from deception.

The word *prosecho* is the compound of two words: the word *pros*, which means *to lean toward*, and the word *echo*, which means *to embrace*. In the context of this verse, the word *prosecho* describes those who are *leaning in a new direction to embrace new ideas*. These people are eager to be open-minded, but the new thinking they are leaning toward doesn't line up with the truth of Scripture.

Paul said what they were leaning toward was "fables" — the Greek word *muthos*, which describes *a myth or fantasy*. It is where we get the word "mythology." These are *stories told in replacement of truth*. In the New Testament, it depicts *false teaching perpetrated in place of truth*.

In addition to "fables," Paul also urged them to avoid "endless genealogies." The word "endless" is the Greek word *aperantos*, and it describes *endless, unbridled, unrestrained thinking*. It is *thinking without any barriers;*

unfounded thoughts; incomplete in content and thought. By using the word *aperantos* — translated here as "endless" — the Holy Spirit is saying that these false teachers were not thinking all the way through the subjects they were teaching.

For example, there are a number of ministers in the pulpit today who don't realize it, but they are teaching doctrine that ultimately leads to *universalism.* This is the errant belief that eventually everyone is going to be saved and reconciled to God — even the devil himself. It insinuates that there was no need for Jesus to die because all paths lead to Heaven. These errant teachers are just looking at a partial doctrine in front of them and not thinking through to where it will end.

The apostle Paul said these fables and endless genealogies "minister questions" to the hearers. The word "minister" is the Greek word *parecho,* which means *gives rise to; brings about; leads to; produces.* In this case, they *give rise to* and *lead to* "questions" — the Greek word *ekdzeteseis,* which describes *unsolvable research; unfounded conclusions; a nonstop seeking for answers that leads to nowhere.* In other words, the telling of fables and endless genealogies produces nothing solid on which you can build your life. These pseudo truths are in constant movement. They are unsolvable and unfounded and leave the listener seeking for answers they will never find.

God's Word Is the Architectural Plan for Your Life

Looking once more at Paul's instruction in First Timothy 1:4, it says, "Neither give heed to fables and endless genealogies, which minister questions, rather than godly edifying which is in faith: so do." Notice the word "edifying." It is the Greek word *oikonomia,* which is *an architectural term meaning to enlarge or amplify a house.* It depicts *the careful following of an architectural plan to enlarge, increase, or amplify.* It also pictures the acts of *edifying; improving; leaving something in an improved condition.*

The God-ordained *architectural plan* we have been given is "the faith." That is, the inspired Word of God has been provided *to enlarge, increase, and amplify* our lives. If we will operate according to the plan of Scripture and not question it, change it, or veer from it, it will *edify* us and *leave us in an improved condition.* That is the dynamic power of God's Word!

Paul then says, "Now the end of the commandment is charity out of a pure heart, and of a good conscience, and of faith unfeigned" (1 Timothy 1:5). Here, we discover the fruit of good teaching: a pure heart, a good conscience, and strong faith. These are what you can expect to experience in your life when you consume the uncontaminated spiritual food of Scripture. We will focus more on this in the coming lessons.

The voice of Scripture is the immutable voice of God. Unfortunately, what is being preached and taught on TV and in many churches today is primarily inspirational and motivational messages. Sound biblical teaching is missing. It is no wonder Paul, Peter, Jude, and Jesus all told us to stand by truth and not allow it to be amended or modified. Cultural norms and people's opinions will always change, but the Bible never changes. It is the *truth*, the *whole truth*, and *nothing but the truth*!

STUDY QUESTIONS

> **Study to shew thyself approved unto God, a workman that needeth not to be ashamed, rightly dividing the word of truth.**
> **— 2 Timothy 2:15**

1. In Second Timothy 3:15-17, the apostle Paul shares the value and vital importance of the Scriptures. Take a moment to read this passage and write out verses 16 and 17. (Also *consider* 1 Peter 2:2; Psalm 119:103; Jeremiah 15:16.)

2. Have you ever gotten spiritual indigestion from teaching that didn't set right with you? Read and commit to memory Paul's powerful words of wisdom in Colossians 2:8.

PRACTICAL APPLICATION

> **But be ye doers of the word, and not hearers only, deceiving your own selves.**
> **— James 1:22**

Every day you are feeding your soul and spirit with the things you take in through your eyes and ears. Every Internet site you surf, every post or blog you read, every movie or TV show you watch, and every song you hear all have a definite level on influence on your life.

1. Be honest. Is there anything you're consuming right now that you know you need to eliminate from your spiritual diet?

2. Are you regularly consuming the life-giving nourishment of God's Word? If so, what has been the best way(s) for you to take in the truth of Scripture and hide it in your heart?

3. If you have struggled to feed on God's Word, take a moment right now to pray. Say, "Lord, please forgive me for neglecting Your Word. Show me practical ways I can begin to daily feed on truth so I can grow in You. Cultivate in me a genuine desire to be in relationship with You. In Jesus' name." Be still and listen. What is the Holy Spirit speaking to you?

LESSON 8

TOPIC

How To Judge if a Teaching Is Good or Bad

SCRIPTURES

1. **1 Timothy 4:1** — Now the Spirit speaketh expressly, that in the latter times some shall depart from the faith, giving heed to seducing spirits and doctrines of demons.

2. **1 Timothy 1:3** — As I besought thee to abide still at Ephesus that thou mightest charge some that they teach no other doctrine.

3. **1 Timothy 1:5** — Now the end of the commandment is charity out of a pure heart, and of a good conscience, and of faith unfeigned.

GREEK WORDS

1. "besought" — **παρακαλέω** (*parakaleo*): to urge, beseech, beg, or even encourage; often used by military leaders or commanding officers before they sent their troops into battle

2. "mightest charge" — **παραγγέλλω** (*parangello*): to order, charge, or give a command; to strictly charge; it is a direct command

3. "other doctrine" — **ἑτεροδιδασκαλέω** (*heterodidaskaleo*): a compound of **ἕτερος** (*heteros*) and **διδάσκαλος** (*didaskalos*); the word **ἕτερος** (*heteros*) points to something of a different kind, and the word **διδάσκαλος** (*didaskalos*) depicts doctrine or teaching; compounded,

ἑτεροδιδασκαλέω (*heterodidaskaleo*) means to teach another doctrine; pictures a doctrine of a different kind or a teaching of a different sort

4. "give heed" — προσέχω (*prosecho*): to embrace

5. "fables" — μῦθος (*muthos*): a myth or fantasy; stories told in replacement of truth; in the New Testament, it depicts false teaching perpetrated in place of truth

6. "endless" — ἀπέραντος (*aperantos*): endless; unbridled; unrestrained; unfounded; incomplete in content and thought

7. "ministers" — παρέχω (*parecho*): gives rise to; brings about; leads to

8. "questions" — ἐκζητήσεις (*ekdzeteseis*): unsolvable research; unfounded conclusions; a nonstop seeking for answers that leads to nowhere

9. "edifying" — οἰκονομία (*oikonomia*): an architectural term meaning to enlarge or amplify a house; it depicts the careful following of an architectural plan to enlarge, increase,or amplify; depicts edifying; improving; leaving something in an improved condition

10. "end" — τέλος (*telos*): goal; principal aim; depicts maturation

11. "commandment" — παραγγελία (*parangelia*):authorized and official teaching

12. "charity" — ἀγάπη (*agape*): a divine love that gives and gives, even if it's never responded to, thanked, or acknowledged; a love for a person or object that is irresistible; a love so profound that it knows no limits or boundaries in how far, wide, high, and deep it will go to show that love to its recipient; a self-sacrificial love that moves the lover to action

13. "pure heart" — καθαρός (*katharos*): purged; cleansed; free of defect; blameless; innocent; free from every admixture of what is false

14. "conscience" — συνείδησις (*suneidesis*): a coming together of all the pieces; understanding; describes seeing the full picture

15. "unfeigned" — ἀνυπόκριτος (*anupokritos*): authentic, genuine; opposite of something pretended, simulated, faked, feigned, or phony; depicts one who is authentic, sincere, or trustworthy

SYNOPSIS

In the ancient city of Ephesus, Curetes Street was the central and most historic thoroughfare in the entire city. Covered colonnades lined both sides of the avenue. These porches, or porticos, were supported by decorated marble columns with terracotta roofs, and the walkways featured fabulous mosaics, many of which are still preserved from the First Century. If you could go back in time and view this street, you would see wealthy people eating at quaint cafes and restaurants while others meandered in and out of shops and bustled about. Indeed, Ephesus was a vibrant city bustling with life.

Right in the middle of all this activity was the church of Ephesus. It was founded by the apostle Paul and his missionary companions Aquila and Priscilla. And just as the city was filled with pagan life, the church was afire with the life and light of God. But not long after Paul had installed Timothy as the pastor of the congregation, a certain number of well-known and beloved leaders began to slowly, subtly embrace false doctrine. In response, Paul wrote to Timothy urging him to take action, giving him guidelines on how to distinguish between good and bad teaching.

The emphasis of this lesson:

Although bad teaching may be interesting and entertaining, it doesn't add to your life and could, in fact, cost you dearly. Good teaching, on the other hand, produces life-giving effects in you.

A Review of Our Foundational Verse

In the First Century, the devil was assaulting the Gospel throughout the Church world, including the church of Ephesus. To help Timothy and his congregants keep their heads on straight, the Holy Spirit prophesied through Paul in First Timothy 4:1, saying, "Now the Spirit speaketh expressly, that in the latter times some shall depart from the faith, giving heed to seducing spirits and doctrines of demons."

As we have seen, the word "latter" is the Greek word *husteros*, and it describes *the ultimate end of a thing with nothing left over*. And the word "times" is the Greek word *kairos*, which means *a season*. Thus, the Spirit said when we come to the very outer edge of the last days and little to no time remains, "seducing spirits, and doctrines of devils" are going to invade the world and permeate society with deception.

The word "doctrines" in this verse is the Greek word *didaskalia*, and it describes *a well-packaged teaching; a sophisticated idea; progressive thinking*. The use of this word indicates that when the enemy invades a belief system, his messages sound very enticing. We're seeing this all around us today. People are believing things that are totally unfounded. Many live their lives guided by their own personal rendition of truth. This has created a breeding ground for Satan to get people to accept whatever lies he desires.

As believers, we are not to be deceived. Just because society is swallowing nonsense, doesn't mean we have to descend into the same lunacy. This was the exact message Paul was trying to convey to Timothy and believers in the First-Century Church.

Paul Instructed Timothy To Reprimand Errant Teachers

Out of great concern for God's people, Paul wrote to Timothy, the pastor of the church of Ephesus, and said, "As I besought thee to abide still at Ephesus…that thou mightest charge some that they teach no other doctrine" (1 Timothy 1:3).

As noted in previous lessons, the word "besought" is the Greek word *parakaleo*, which means *to urge; to beseech; to beg*. It is also a word for *prayer*, and, as such, it depicts Paul on his knees *begging* and *pleading* with Timothy to take his responsibility seriously and bring correction to the notable leaders who had veered off course. This job of correction was clearly not something Timothy was excited about doing — hence, the reason Paul *begged* him to do it.

Next, notice the phrase "mightest charge." This is the Greek word *parangello*, which means *to order*, *to strictly charge*, or *to give a command*. In other words, Paul didn't tell Timothy to give a *suggestion* to these false teachers; he wanted him to give them a very direct command to them to stop their errant teaching.

Now Paul did not say that *every* leader in Ephesus had fallen prey to seducing spirits and doctrines of demons. He stated that only "some" had succumbed to it. This word "some" is the Greek word *tisin*, which describes *a certain some; a notable some; certain ones*. The same is true regarding the end times in which we're living today. Not everyone will be led astray. Thankfully, many leaders will stick with the truth and refuse to budge from it.

Nevertheless, that Bible says *a notable some* were teaching "other doctrine," which is the Greek word *heterodidaskaleo*. It is a compound of the words *heteros* and *didaskalos*. The word *heteros* points to *something of a different sort*, and the word *didaskalos* depicts *sophisticated doctrine or teaching*. When these words are compounded, it means *a doctrine of a different kind* or *a teaching of a different sort*. Paul was saying, "What they're teaching may sound like sophisticated, sound doctrine, but it is not. It's *heteros* — it has been modified, and it is not the same doctrine we gave you."

People Were Wandering From the Fundamentals of the Faith

Paul added to his instruction in First Timothy 1:4, saying, "Neither give heed to fables and endless genealogies, which minister questions, rather than godly edifying which is in faith: so do." The phrase "give heed" is the Greek word *prosecho*, which is a compound of the word *pros*, meaning *toward*, and the word *echo*, meaning *to embrace*. The word *prosecho* is a picture of *someone who is releasing what was once precious and dear to embrace a new system of thinking*. This is actually the same word used by Jesus in Matthew 24 and used by Paul in First Timothy 4:1 to describe the activity of *seducing spirits*.

The truth is, people are "giving heed" (*prosecho*) to erroneous teaching all over the world today. They are wandering from the most basic fundamentals of the faith. This is especially true of the younger generation who are totally uninformed of central Bible doctrines, such as the virgin birth, the sinless nature of Christ, and the need for repentance. The reason they don't understand these truths is a result of not being properly taught.

In Paul's day, he said many were embracing "fables," which is the Greek word *muthos*. It is where we get the word "mythology," and it describes *a myth or fantasy; stories told in replacement of truth*. In the New Testament, it depicts *false teaching perpetrated in place of truth*.

In addition to fables, Paul said people were also giving heed to "endless genealogies" The word "endless" here is the Greek word *aperantos*, which means *endless; unbridled; unrestrained; unfounded; incomplete in content and thought*. This word depicts people who just aren't thinking things through completely.

What was the result of people hearing fables and endless genealogies? Paul stated they did "minister questions" to the listeners. In Greek, the word "minster" is the word *parecho*, which means *gives rise to; brings about;*

leads to. Fables and endless genealogies gave rise to "questions." In the Greek, this word describes *unsolvable research; unfounded conclusions; a nonstop seeking for answers that leads to nowhere.*

Paul said that instead of fables and endless genealogies, teachers were to impart what was "edifying" (*see* 1 Timothy 1:4). The word "edifying" is the Greek word *oikonomia,* which is *an architectural term meaning to enlarge or amplify a house.* It depicts *the careful following of an architectural plan to enlarge, increase, amplify, edify, or improve.*

Only God's Word provides a solid, stable foundation on which a person can build his or her life. Everything else is shifting sand. The Bible will build your marriage, your family, your business, and every other part of your life. So instead of listening to unfounded nonsense, stick with Scripture.

Great Results Come From Receiving Solid Biblical Teaching

Paul followed up his instructions to Timothy in First Timothy1:3,4 with this statement: "Now the end of the commandment is charity out of a pure heart, and of a good conscience, and of faith unfeigned" (v. 5). The word "end" in this verse is the Greek word *telos,* which describes *a goal* or *a principal aim.* And the word "commandment" in Greek is the word *parangelia,* and it describes *authorized and official teaching.* Thus, if teaching has really come from the throne of God, it is *authorized and official.* Taking these meanings into account, the beginning of this verse could better be translated, "Now the *goal* of the *authorized and official teaching…*" or, "… The *principal aim* of the *authorized and official teaching….*"

When the authorized truth of Scripture is taught, the first thing it provides is "charity." The word "charity" is the Greek word *agape.* It describes *a divine love that gives and gives, even if it's never responded to, thanked, or acknowledged.* It pictures *a love for a person or object that is irresistible; a love so profound that it knows no limits or boundaries in how far, wide, high, and deep it will go to show that love to its recipient.* It is *a self-sacrificial love that moves the lover to action.* Thus, when you are receiving good Bible teaching, it will greatly improve your love walk.

The second positive effect of hearing and receiving uncontaminated truth is a "pure heart." The word "pure" is the Greek word *katharos.* It is where we get the word "catheterize." It means *purged; cleansed; free of defect; blameless; innocent; free from every admixture of what is false.* When people are admitted into the hospital, they are often catheterized. This allows toxins to continually drain from the body so that it can fully heal. In the same way, when you receive the Word of God, it catheterizes your heart and allows whatever toxins are present to be expelled.

The third blessing that results from receiving the pure Word of God is a "good conscience." First Timothy 1:5 says, "Now the end of the commandment is charity out of a pure heart, and of a good conscience...." The word "conscience" in this passage is the Greek word *suneidesis*, and it describes *a coming together of all the pieces; understanding.* When people first come to Christ, they receive bits and pieces of understanding regarding their salvation and relationship with God. Over time as they feed on the truth of Scripture, the Holy Spirit expands their understanding, giving them a fuller, more detailed picture of God's Word and their relationship with Him.

The fourth benefit of hearing and receiving sound biblical teaching is "faith unfeigned." The word "unfeigned" is the Greek word *anupokritos*, and it describes *something authentic or genuine.* It is the opposite of something *pretended, simulated, faked, feigned, or phony.* It *depicts one who is authentic, sincere, or trustworthy.* When you feed on sound, biblical teaching, it will create in you an authentic faith that pleases the Lord.

STUDY QUESTIONS

> Study to shew thyself approved unto God, a workman that needeth not to be ashamed, rightly dividing the word of truth.
> — 2 Timothy 2:15

1. Take a few moments to review First Timothy 1:4 and the Greek meanings of its key words presented in this lesson. In your own words, describe the *negative* effects of receiving *bad* teaching?
2. Step back and take an honest inventory of your life. Are you experiencing any of these negative side effects? If so, which one(s)?
3. Now carefully read through First Timothy 1:5 and the Greek meanings of its key words presented in this lesson. In your own words, describe the *blessings* of receiving *good* teaching?

4. Which of these blessings have you personally experienced? What practical steps can you take to enjoy more of this fruit of good teaching in your life?

PRACTICAL APPLICATION

> But be ye doers of the word, and not hearers only, deceiving your own selves.
> —James 1:22

1. One of the blessings of receiving solid biblical teaching is a good "conscience," which in Greek describes *a coming together of all the pieces; understanding; the ability to see the full picture.* In what ways has the Holy Spirit brought this about in your life? What has He revealed to you that has helped deepen and expand your understanding of Him and His Word?

2. The pure teaching of Scripture is "edifying" — it is God's *architectural plan to enlarge, increase, and improve your life.* In what areas of your life do you need and want to experience edifying? Using a Bible concordance or online search, look up scriptures on these topics that you can meditate on and feed your spirit.

LESSON 9

TOPIC

The Goal of Good Teaching

SCRIPTURES

1. **1 Timothy 4:1** — Now the Spirit speaketh expressly, that in the latter times some shall depart from the faith, giving heed to seducing spirits and doctrines of demons.

2. **1 Timothy 1:3** — As I besought thee to abide still at Ephesus that thou mightest charge some that they teach no other doctrine.

3. **1 Timothy 1:7** — Desiring to be teachers of the law; understanding neither what they say, nor whereof they affirm.

4. **Hebrews 5:12** — For when for the time ye ought to be teachers, ye have need that one teach you again which be the first principles of the

oracles of God; and are become such as have need of milk, and not of strong meat.

GREEK WORDS

1. "besought" — παρακαλέω (*parakaleo*): to urge, beseech, beg, or even encourage; often used by military leaders or commanding officers before they sent their troops into battle

2. "other doctrine" — ἑτεροδιδασκαλέω (*heterodidaskaleo*): a compound of ἕτερος (*heteros*) and διδάσκαλος (*didaskalos*); the word ἕτερος (*heteros*) points to something of a different kind, and the word διδάσκαλος (*didaskalos*) depicts doctrine or teaching; compounded, ἑτεροδιδασκαλέω (*heterodidaskaleo*) means to teach another doctrine; pictures a doctrine of a different kind or a teaching of a different sort

3. "desiring" — θέλω (*thelo*): to earnestly desire; to long for; depicts an earnest, ongoing desire

4. "teachers of the law" — νομοδιδάσκαλος (*nomodidaskalos*): a compound of νόμος (*nomos*) and διδάσκαλος (*didaskalos*); the word νόμος (*nomos*) means rules, principles, or the unchanging and unbendable rule of faith; διδάσκαλος (*didaskalos*) refers to a masterful teacher; compounded, νομοδιδάσκαλος (*nomodidaskalos*) pictures a masterful scripture-lawyer; someone scholarly in interpreting the Bible

5. "understanding" — νοοῦντες (*noountes*): a derivative of the word νοῦς (*nous*); to perceive; refers to the mind and the ability to think, reason, understand, and comprehend; pictures the place where reasoning, perception, and understanding takes place

6. "they say" — λέγουσιν (*legousin*): to repeatedly say, over and over

7. "affirm" — διαβεβαιόομαι (*diabebaioomai*): continuous sense that means to continuously assert; to continuously try to establish or affirm confidently

8. "ought" — ὀφείλω (*opheilo*): to owe; pictures an obligation or necessity; something that should be achieved or accomplished; something that is owed; a moral duty

9. "teachers" — διδάσκαλοι (*didaskaloi*): masterful teachers; those superior in their field of expertise; rabbis

10. "need" — χρεία (*chreia*): a deficit; a need that must be met

11. "teach" — διδάσκω (*didasko*): to teach; pictures a systematic learning of a student through the ever-present instruction of a teacher

12. "first" — ἀρχῆς (*arches*): the first; the beginning; something that is elementary

13. "principles" — στοιχεῖον (*stoicheion*): basic elements; fundamentals; rudimentary knowledge essential before advancing to higher education; foundational knowledge

SYNOPSIS

The apostle Paul spent several years establishing the church of Ephesus, and one of his major endeavors during that time was to teach solid Bible doctrine. He did this daily at the lecture hall known as the School of Tyrannus (*see* Acts 19:9). From that location, the Word of God literally spread throughout the entire Roman province of Asia. Decades later, in about 110 AD, under the rule of Emperor Trajan, the Celsus Library was built near the same location. It became one of the largest libraries in the ancient world, providing people with a plethora of materials to read and enhance their education. Indeed, the value of education should never be diminished — including spiritual education. The practice of reading and studying Scripture is priceless. When you have a solid understanding of the Word of God, you can readily recognize and avoid the enemy's deadly deceptions.

The emphasis of this lesson:

In order to rightly divide the Scriptures and accurately apply them to our lives, we must have a solid understanding of the fundamentals of the faith. A sincere desire alone is not enough.

When the apostle Paul heard that well-known teachers in the church of Ephesus were beginning to stray from the truth of Scripture and teach false doctrines, he wrote Timothy and said, "As I besought thee to abide still at Ephesus...that thou mightest charge some that they teach no other doctrine" (1 Timothy 1:3).

We have learned that the word "besought" is the Greek word *parakaleo*, which means *to urge, to beseech, to beg*, or *to plead*. Interestingly, this word was also often used by military leaders or commanding officers before they sent their troops into battle. By using this word, Paul was not only begging Timothy to deal with errant teachers and to set them straight, he was also notifying him of the battle for doctrine that was in front of him.

The phrase "that thou mightiest charge" in Greek means that Timothy was *to issue a direct command* to the notable some to "teach no other doctrine." The phrase "other doctrine" is the Greek word *heterodidaskaleo*. It is a compound of the word *heteros*, which means *something of a different sort*, and the word *didaskalos*, which depicts *masterful doctrine or teaching*. When these words are compounded, it describes *a doctrine of a different kind* or *a teaching of a different sort*. These individuals were teaching a creed that did not match the authentic teaching of Scripture, and it needed to stop.

Accurate Knowledge of the Truth Is Needed To Fulfill Godly Desire

In Paul's instructions to Timothy, it appears as though he was giving the benefit of the doubt to those who were teaching errant doctrine. His words reveal he believed they were sincere, but sometimes people can be sincere in their beliefs and be sincerely wrong in what they are doing.

In First Timothy 1:7, Paul said, "Desiring to be teachers of the law; understanding neither what they say, nor whereof they affirm." The word "desiring" in this verse is the Greek word *thelo*, which means *to earnestly desire; to long for*. The tense here depicts *an earnest, ongoing or perpetual desire*. It is a longing that consumes one's attention and energy. And the desire these individuals had was to be "teachers of the law."

The phrase "teachers of the law" is the Greek word *nomodidaskalos* — a word that only appears three times in the New Testament. It is a compound of the word *nomos* and *didaskalos*. The word *nomos* means *rules, principles, or the unchanging and unbendable rule of faith*. It is where we get the word "law." And the word *didaskalos* refers to *a masterful teacher; a masterful scripture-lawyer; someone scholarly in interpreting the Bible*. These people had a sincere desire to be scholarly and speak with great authority. However, they had a problem: Something was askew in their thinking.

Paul stated they were "…understanding neither what they say, nor whereof they affirm." The word "understanding" in Greek is the term *noountes*, which is a derivative of the word *nous*, the word for *the mind*. This word refers to *the ability to think, to reason, to understand, and to comprehend; the place where reasoning, perception, and understanding takes place*. The phrase "understanding neither" indicates there was something defective or faulty in the way they were reasoning — they were not thinking through the ramifications of what they were teaching.

Paul noted that the things they were saying were in error. The phrase "they say" in First Timothy 1:7 is the Greek word *legousin*, which means *repeatedly saying over and over*. Paul said these false teachers didn't understand "…what they say, nor what they affirm." The word "affirm" in Greek is the word *diabebaioomai*, and it depicts *a continuous sense that means to continuously assert; to continuously try to establish or affirm confidently*.

Thus, Paul said these individuals were longing with desire to be scholarly teachers of the law, but they were very defective in their thinking and reasoning. Again and again, they repeatedly tried to establish their "new ideas," but their concepts had no foundation or roots.

Many people today are doing the same thing. For instance, some leaders are attempting to teach things such as: 1) there is no hell; 2) repentance for sin is no longer necessary; and 3) sin doesn't exist. But they have no scriptural foundation for these lines of thinking. If they would simply take their theory, search the Scriptures, and think it all the way through to its ultimate outcome, they would see that what they're teaching is totally unfounded in God's Word.

A Thorough Understanding of Bible Basics Is Vital

It is God's Word, *and God's Word alone*, that provides a solid foundation for all doctrine and standards for living. The writer of Hebrews noted this in Hebrews 5:12: "For when for the time ye ought to be teachers, ye have need that one teach you again which be the first principles of the oracles of God; and are become such as have need of milk, and not of strong meat."

The word "ought" in this verse is the Greek word *opheilo*, which means *to owe*. It pictures *an obligation or necessity; something that should be achieved or accomplished; something that is owed; a moral duty*. And the word "teachers" in Greek is *didaskaloi*, which describes *masterful teachers; those superior in their field of expertise; rabbis*. Hence, a better translation of the phrase "ye ought to be teachers" would be, "You are obligated to be teachers. After all you've seen and heard and all the information you've had at your disposal, you really should have achieved the status of a masterful teacher or rabbi."

Next, notice the word "need." It is the Greek word *chreia*, and it describes *a deficit; a need that must be met*. After noting that the Hebrews should have been masterful teachers, the writer identified a glaring deficit in their lives: they lacked accurate understanding of the foundations of the faith and needed someone to teach them.

This brings us to the word "teach" — the Greek word *didasko*, which means *to teach*. It pictures *a systematic learning of a student through the ever-present instruction of a teacher*. In history, the teacher would sit right by his student to instruct him. Basically, the recipients of this letter from Paul were being told, "You need someone to take you to school and sit with you until you get it."

In what did the Hebrews need to be schooled? "The first principles of the oracles of God." The word "first" is the Greek word *arches*, and it means *the first; the beginning; something that is elementary*. And the word "principles" in Greek is the word *stoicheion*, and it describes *the basic elements; fundamentals; rudimentary knowledge essential before advancing to higher education*.

Consider this example. Before a surgeon begins practicing medicine and operating on patients, he must spend many years being educated. If a young adolescent said, "I really want to be a brain surgeon," no one would place a scalpel in his hand and send him into the operating room just because he had a sincere desire to be a doctor. First, he would have to finish high school, complete college, graduate from medical school, and learn all the fundamentals of medicine and the human body. Until he finished his education and a trial period of residency, he would not be elevated to the office of surgeon.

The same is true for us spiritually. In order to accurately impart the Word, those who desire to be teachers need to be sufficiently schooled and trained in the knowledge of Scripture, starting with the fundamental ABCs of the Bible.

STUDY QUESTIONS

> **Study to shew thyself approved unto God, a workman that needeth not to be ashamed, rightly dividing the word of truth.**
> **— 2 Timothy 2:15**

1. The Holy Spirit, writing through the apostle Paul, gives us a power principle for living in Second Timothy 2:15. Take a moment to write out this verse and commit it to memory. (Also *consider* Romans 12:2; Colossians 3:16.)

2. How important is it for you and your children and your children's children to really know the Word of God? Read Deuteronomy 11:18-21 for the answer. (Also *consider* the wisdom of Psalm 78:1-8.)

3. What blessings can you expect from studying Scripture, and in what practical ways can you obey these instructions from the Lord in your day-to-day living?

PRACTICAL APPLICATION

> But be ye doers of the word, and not hearers only,
> deceiving your own selves.
> —James 1:22

1. Before you move on to the deeper truths of the Christian faith, it is imperative that you have a solid grasp on the fundamentals. What would you say are some of the vital, non-negotiable ABCs of the faith? (*Consider* Hebrews 6:1,2.) How well would you say that you know these?

2. In First Timothy 1:7, it appears as though Paul chose to believe the best of the people who were teaching error, assuming their motives were sincere. Why is it not our place to judge people's motives? (For help, *see* 1 Corinthians 4:5.)

LESSON 10

TOPIC

What Happens When Someone Swerves From the Truth

SCRIPTURES

1. **1 Timothy 4:1** — Now the Spirit speaketh expressly, that in the latter times some shall depart from the faith, giving heed to seducing spirits and doctrines of demons.

2. **1 Timothy 1:3,4** — As I besought thee to abide still at Ephesus that thou mightest charge some that they teach no other doctrine. Neither

give heed to fables and endless genealogies, which minster questions, rather than godly edifying which is in faith: so do.

3. **1 Timothy 1:5** — Now the end of the commandment is charity out of a pure heart, and of a good conscience, and of faith unfeigned. From which some having swerved have turned aside unto vain jangling.

GREEK WORDS

1. "besought" — **παρακαλέω** (*parakaleo*): to urge, beseech, beg, or even encourage; often used by military leaders or commanding officers before they sent their troops into battle

2. "other doctrine" — **ἑτεροδιδασκαλέω** (*heterodidaskaleo*): a compound of **ἕτερος** (*heteros*) and **διδάσκαλος** (*didaskalos*); the word **ἕτερος** (*heteros*) points to something of a different kind, and the word **διδάσκαλος** (*didaskalos*) depicts doctrine or teaching; compounded, **ἑτεροδιδασκαλέω** (*heterodidaskaleo*) means to teach another doctrine; pictures a doctrine of a different kind or a teaching of a different sort

3. "give heed" — **προσέχω** (*prosecho*): to embrace

4. "fables" — **μῦθος** (*muthos*): a myth or fantasy; stories told in replacement of truth; in the New Testament, depicts false teaching perpetrated in place of truth

5. "endless" — **ἀπέραντος** (*aperantos*): endless; unbridled; unrestrained; unfounded; incomplete in content and thought

6. "minister" — **παρέχω** (*parecho*): gives rise to; brings about; leads to

7. "questions" — **ἐκζητήσεις** (*ekdzeteseis*): unsolvable research; unfounded conclusions; a nonstop seeking for answers that leads to nowhere

8. "edifying" — **οἰκονομία** (*oikonomia*): an architectural term meaning to enlarge or amplify a house; depicts the careful following of an architectural plan to enlarge, increase, or amplify; depicts edifying; improving; leaving something in an improved condition

9. "end" — **τέλος** (*telos*): goal; principal aim; depicts maturation

10. "commandment" — **παραγγελία** (*parangelia*): authorized and official teaching

11. "charity" — **ἀγάπη** (*agape*): a divine love that gives and gives, even if it's never responded to, thanked, or acknowledged; a love for a person or object that is irresistible; a love so profound that it knows no limits or boundaries in how far, wide, high, and deep it will go to show that love to its recipient; a self-sacrificial love that moves the lover to action

12. "pure heart" — καθαρός (*katharos*): purged; cleansed; free of defect; blameless; innocent; free from every admixture of what is false

13. "conscience" — συνείδησις (*suneidesis*): a coming together of all the pieces; understanding; describes seeing the full picture

14. "unfeigned" — ἀνυπόκριτος (*anupokritos*): authentic; genuine; opposite of something pretended, simulated, faked, feigned, or phony; depicts one who is authentic, sincere, or trustworthy

15. "swerved" — ἀστοχέω (*astocheo*): to miss the mark; to be off target; to be out of line; or to deviate from the goal or truth

16. "turned aside" — ἐκτρέπω (*ektrepo*): to turn away; also, a medical term that describes a bone out of joint; depicts wandering from an originally intended location; a mutation into something different than was originally intended

17. "vain jangling" — ματαιολογία (*mataiologia*): wasted talk; empty words; foolish, nonsensical talk; useless chatter

SYNOPSIS

There are two important streets that intersect in the city of Ephesus — Curetes Street and Marble Street. This was at one time the most prestigious corner in the entire city. As people traveled through the region, they would often arrive at this junction and accidentally go the wrong way. Their directional error would take them far off track from their intended destination.

That is precisely what happens to us when we swerve off course doctrinally. What may seem like a tiny turn in the wrong direction can greatly impact our course and cause us to end up far from where we are supposed to be. Therefore, it is imperative to stay on track with truth by knowing the God's Word.

The emphasis of this lesson:

Deviating from the divine truth of God's Word is hazardous to your spiritual health.

'In Latter Times Some Will Depart From the Faith'

Looking again at our foundational scripture in First Timothy 4:1, Paul wrote, "Now the Spirit speaketh expressly, that in the latter times some shall depart from the faith, giving heed to seducing spirits and doctrines of devils."

In this verse, the Holy Spirit tells us what will happen in the "latter times." The word "latter" here is the Greek word *husteros*, and it describes *the very ultimate end of a thing, when nothing is left over*. The fact that this verse includes the word "times" — the Greek word *kairos*, which means *a season* — indicates that the Spirit is pointing to the very end of the age. It is the timeframe in which we are now living.

During these last of the last days, the Lord says, "…Some shall depart from the faith." The phrase "the faith" is significant. In Greek, it includes the definite article. Hence, it is not faith for signs and wonders or faith for miracles and healings. It is "the faith," which points specifically to the timeless teaching of God's Word. At the very end of the age, people are going to depart from the soundness of Scripture.

The word "depart" is the Greek word *aphistemi*, which describes *a very slow, gradual movement away from what was once held to be precious and dear*. In this case, it is a step-by-step withdrawal from the absolute truth of Scripture. We are seeing this happen today. More and more, the Bible is being viewed as an ancient relic that is no longer relevant to resolve the issues of modern times. Thus, many people are left to come to their own conclusions.

As people drift away from the truth of God's Word, First Timothy 4:1 says they begin "…giving heed to seducing spirits and doctrines of devils." The phrase "giving heed" is the Greek word *prosecho*, which means *to lean toward and embrace something new*. Although there is nothing wrong with being open-minded, we need to be careful not to be so open-minded that we lose our grip on sound teaching. God has given us the gift of a sound mind, and He wants us to fill it with the accurate knowledge of His Word and to think through things wisely.

'Other Doctrine' Was Causing People To Swerve Off Course

When Paul wrote to Timothy, he also said, "As I besought thee to abide still at Ephesus…that thou mightest charge some that they teach no other doctrine" (1 Timothy 1:3). The phrase "teach no other doctrine" lets us know what was going on inside the church of Ephesus.

There was a group of well-known and greatly loved leaders there who had influence and a reputation. The Bible refers to them using the word "some," which is the Greek word *tisen*, meaning *a notable some or certain ones*. These individuals were using their positions to influence others, leading them away from truth and into error.

The Bible says they were teaching "other doctrine," which we've seen is the Greek word *heterodidaskaleo*. It is a compound of the word *heteros* and *didaskalos*; the word *heteros* points to *something of a different kind*, and the word *didaskalos* depicts *doctrine or teaching*. When the two words are compounded to form the word *heterodidaskaleo*, it means *to teach another doctrine*, and it pictures *a doctrine of a different kind* or *a teaching of a different sort*.

What was being taught in the church of Ephesus was well-developed and well-presented, but it was not the authentic, sound doctrine that the Holy Spirit had taught through Paul and Timothy in the foundational years of the church. It was a diversion. And if a powerhouse church like Ephesus that really knew the truth could veer off course, then we can veer off course as well.

'Fables and Endless Genealogies' Replaced Truth

In First Timothy 1:4, Paul continued his words of warning, saying "Neither give heed to fables and endless genealogies, which minster questions, rather than godly edifying which is in faith: so do." The phrase "give heed" is the same Greek word we saw in First Timothy 4:1 where Paul talked about "giving heed to seducing spirits and doctrines of devils." It is the word *prosecho*. Only in this verse, he refers to not giving heed to "fables and endless genealogies."

The word "fables" is the Greek word *muthos*, which is from where we get the word *mythology*. The word *muthos* describes *a myth or fantasy*. These are *stories told in replacement of truth*. In the New Testament, the word *muthos* depicts *false teaching perpetrated in place of truth*. So instead of solid preaching grounded in Scripture, teaching that resembled fictional mythology took its place.

To this description, Paul added the phrase "endless genealogies." The word "endless" is the Greek word *aperantos*, and it describes *something endless; unbridled; unrestrained; unfounded; incomplete in content and thought*. By using this word, Paul lets us know that people were teaching ideas without thinking all the way through to where those ideas would lead them. In other words, there was no end in mind.

The Same Thing Is Happening Today

Certain leaders are teaching ideas and concepts without thinking through to where those ideas will ultimately bring a person. For instance, there are individuals who are espousing there is no hell and that hell has never existed. They argue that God is so rich in mercy and love that He accepts and forgives everyone. However, if that is true, there would have been no need for Christ to die and no purpose in preaching the Gospel. To teach there is no hell is unscriptural and potentially detrimental to one's eternity.

There are also many people today who question the issue of gender — even in the Church. The very foundational truth that we are created "in the image of God, male and female" (*see* Genesis 1:27) is up for grabs in their minds. Again, the reason for questioning gender is a result of not thinking the concept all the way through to the end.

How about the concept of God's grace? There are several modifications to this vital doctrine that are being taught today, and some are very disturbing. Certain individuals have cunningly turned the grace of God into a license to sin, teaching that grace is God's big "cover-up" for our sins.

Then there are those who advocate we no longer need to teach the Old Testament. They say it is outdated, irrelevant, and for people of a different time. They even endorse disconnecting from the Ten Commandments, asserting it has no application on New Testament believers who are saved by grace.

The problem with all these "new revelations" is that the people who are disseminating them are not thinking their concepts through all the way to discover where its adherents will ultimately end up. Some of these individuals are quite sincere in what they are saying, but they are sincerely wrong. This is the type of doctrine Paul was referring to when he talked about "fables and endless genealogies." It is unrestrained, off track, and comes to illogical conclusions.

When You Stay with Scripture, Your Life Is Edified

What resulted from these fables and endless genealogies? Paul said they "...minster questions, rather than godly edifying which is in faith: so do." The word "minister" in this verse is the Greek word *parecho*, which means *gives rise to; brings about; leads to*. In this case, fables and endless genealogies give rise and lead to "questions" — the Greek word *ekdzeteseis*, which means *unsolvable research; unfounded conclusions; a nonstop seeking for answers that leads to nowhere.*

The goal of good teaching is "godly edifying." The word "edifying" in Greek is the word *oikonomia*, which is *an architectural term meaning to enlarge or amplify a house*. It depicts *the careful following of an architectural plan to enlarge, increase, amplify, edify, or improve*.

When you stay with Scripture, which is God's architectural plan for your life, it transforms you. It *amplifies, enlarges,* and *leaves you in a better condition* than you were in before. That is why the devil fights so furiously to keep you and everyone else from regularly getting into the Word. He would much rather have people hooked on his hallucinations than on the true revelations of Scripture. But if you will stick with God's Word, you will be adequately equipped for victorious living.

The Blessings of Good Bible Teaching

In First Timothy 1:5, Paul specified four blessings that result from receiving good Bible teaching. He said, "Now the end of the commandment is charity out of a pure heart, and of a good conscience, and of faith unfeigned."

As we saw in a previous lesson, the word "end" is the Greek word *telos*, which describes *the goal or principal aim*, and the word "commandment" in the Greek is the word *parangelia*, which denotes *authorized and official teaching*. Essentially, Paul was saying, "The end goal of authorized, official Bible teaching is charity out of a pure heart, a good conscience, and of faith unfeigned."

The word "charity" in this verse is the Greek word *agape*. It is *a divine love that gives and gives, even if it's never responded to, thanked, or acknowledged; a love for a person or object that is irresistible; a love so profound that it knows no limits or boundaries in how far, wide, high, and deep it will go to show that love to its recipient; a self-sacrificial love that moves the lover to action*. This tells us that one of the major blessings resulting from solid Scriptural teaching is an ongoing improvement in your love walk.

The second blessing or good teaching Paul cited is "a pure heart." The phrase "pure heart" is the Greek word *katharos*, which means *purged; cleansed; free of defect; blameless; innocent; free from every admixture of what is false*. The word *katharos* is from where we get the word *catheter*. When someone is admitted to the hospital, they're sometimes catheterized in order for his body to release toxins. In a similar way, when we receive the pure teaching of Scripture, our heart is catheterized in order to drain off any poisons that are present.

A "good conscience" is the third benefit of receiving sound doctrine. The word "conscience" is the Greek word *suneidesis*, and it describes *a coming together of all the pieces; understanding*. When you hear the truth of God's Word, the Holy Spirit begins to put all the pieces together about God, His Word, and your identity in Him. Little by little, he reveals how all the pieces fit together, helping you see the full picture. A "good conscience" depicts a person with a healthy mind working in unity with his spirit.

The fourth blessing Paul noted that accompanies good teaching is "faith unfeigned." The word "unfeigned" is the Greek word *anupokritos*, and it describes something *authentic or genuine*. It the opposite of something *pretended, simulated, faked, feigned, or phony*, and it depicts one who is *authentic, sincere, or trustworthy*. Good Bible teaching will cultivate a genuine, authentic faith in you.

Be Careful Not To Swerve or Turn Aside From Truth

When we come to First Timothy 1:6, Paul talked again about those who have swerved from the teaching of Scripture. He said, "From which some having swerved have turned aside unto vain jangling." The word "swerved" here is the Greek word *astocheo*, which means *to miss the mark; to be off target; to be out of line; or to deviate from the goal or truth*. Sadly, many who have "swerved" from good teaching don't even know the doctrinal mark for which they are aiming because they have not been taught the truth. That is why they are swerving.

Once a person begins swerving, he is then "turned aside" even further. In Greek, "turned aside" is the word *ektrepo*, which is *a medical term that describes a bone out of joint*. Think about it. When someone has a bone out of joint, it affects his whole body. In fact, all that person's attention begins to be focused on that one bone out of place, as it is such a source of pain. This is a picture of what happens when a person becomes "out of joint" doctrinally. Even though that individual saved and still in the Body of Christ, he or she becomes a source of pain and irritation to the whole Church, which can be quite paralyzing.

If a person continues to be out of joint doctrinally and refuses to cooperate with the Holy Spirit's correction, his condition will turn into "vain jangling." This is an old King James phrase translated from the Greek word *mataiologia*, which describes *wasted talk; empty words; foolish, nonsensical talk; useless chatter*. Those who persist at embracing non-biblical ideas and concepts eventually begin to believe and promote "vain jangling," which is essentially nothing but nonsense.

To avoid becoming a dispenser of nonsense and an irritant to those around you, stay intimately connected with the pure truth of God's Word. Know what it teaches and you will not swerve or turn aside from it.

STUDY QUESTIONS

> **Study to shew thyself approved unto God, a workman that needeth not to be ashamed, rightly dividing the word of truth.**
> **— 2 Timothy 2:15**

1. When Jesus was being tempted by the devil in the desert, He quoted a powerful passage from the Old Testament: "…Man shall not live by bread alone, but by every word that proceedeth out of the mouth of God" (Matthew 4:4). What do you understand Jesus to be communicating here in His response to Satan? (Also *consider* Deuteronomy 8:3; Luke 4:4.)

2. Carefully read Jesus' words in John 6:48-58. What does He repeatedly identify Himself as in these verses? How do His words here relate to Deuteronomy 8:3 and Matthew 4:4?

PRACTICAL APPLICATION

> **But be ye doers of the word, and not hearers only, deceiving your own selves.**
> **— James 1:22**

1. In your own words, briefly describe the value of God's Word why it is a priority in your life.

2. If all Bibles were suddenly confiscated and you no longer had access to a written or digital copy of the Word, what would your reaction be? If you knew this was going to happen, would you do anything differently? If so, what?

3. Why do you think it's important to realize that if a powerhouse church like Ephesus could veer off course, then we can easily veer off course as well?

4. One of the blessings of receiving the pure Word of God is a "good conscience." This means the Holy Spirit begins to put all the pieces together about God, His Word, and your identity in Him. How does being able to see the full picture of things encourage and empower you? What do you think are some of the dangers of building doctrine on just pieces of truth?

LESSON 11

TOPIC

Seducing Spirits and Doctrines of Demons

SCRIPTURES

1. **1 Timothy 1:7** — Desiring to be teachers of the law; understanding neither what they say, nor whereof they affirm.

2. **1 Timothy 4:1** — Now the Spirit speaketh expressly, that in the latter times some shall depart from the faith, giving heed to seducing spirits and doctrines of demons.

3. **1 Timothy 4:6** — If thou put the brethren in remembrance of these things, thou shalt be a good minister of Jesus Christ, nourished up in the words of faith and of good doctrine, whereunto thou hast attained.

GREEK WORDS

1. "desiring" — θέλω (*thelo*): to earnestly desire; to long for; depicts an earnest, ongoing desire

2. "teachers of the law" — νομοδιδάσκαλος (*nomodidaskalos*): a compound of νόμος (*nomos*) and διδάσκαλος (*didaskalos*); the word νόμος

(*nomos*) means rules, principles, or the unchanging and unbendable rule of faith; **διδάσκαλος** (*didaskalos*) refers to a masterful teacher; compounded, **νομοδιδάσκαλος** (*nomodidaskalos*) pictures a masterful scripture-lawyer; someone scholarly in interpreting the Bible

3. "understanding" — **νοοῦντες** (*noountes*): a derivative of the word **νοῦς** (*nous*); to perceive; refers to the mind and the ability to think, reason, understand, and comprehend; pictures the place where reasoning, perception, and understanding takes place

4. "they say" — **λέγουσιν** (*legousin*): to repeatedly say, over and over

5. "affirm" — **διαβεβαιόομαι** (*diabebaioomai*): continuous sense that means to continuously assert; to continuously try to establish or affirm confidently

6. "remembrance" — **ὑποτίθημι** (*hupotithemi*): a compound of **ὑπο** (*hupo*) and **τίθημι** (*tithemi*); the word **ὑπο** (*hupo*) means by or under; **τίθημι** (*tithemi*)means to lay, place, or position something, like a foundation; because **τίθημι** (*tithemi*) carries an architectural concept, it can picture one laying a foundation underneath the brethren

SYNOPSIS

One of the most remarkable archaeological sites in the ancient city of Ephesus is the Temple of Serapis. It is located off the beaten path behind the library and the state agora, and it was simply breathtaking in its day. The religion of Serapis originated in Egypt. It was a very eerie, dark cult filled with all kinds of dark occult rituals. Accordingly, the Temple of Serapis was swarming with seducing spirits and doctrines of demons.

The apostle Paul talked about seducing spirits and doctrines of demons infiltrating the Church in the last days. At the very end of the Church age, a number of believers are going to begin withdrawing from the sound doctrine of Scripture and begin embracing doctrines that are dark and sinister. To ensure that we are not led off track in this departure, we must stay grounded in the truth.

The emphasis of this lesson:

The Holy Spirit prophesied through Paul that seducing spirits and doctrines of demons would abound in the last days.

Errant Teachers at Ephesus Modified the Truth

In First Timothy 1:3, the apostle Paul wrote to Timothy, urging him to address the issue of errant teachers in the church of Ephesus. He said, "As I besought thee to abide still at Ephesus, when I went into Macedonia, that thou mightest charge some that they teach no other doctrine."

We have learned that the phrase "other doctrine" is the Greek word *heterodidaskaleo*, which is a compound of the word *heteros* and *didaskalos*. The word *heteros* points to *something of a different kind*, and the word *didaskalos* depicts *sophisticated doctrine or teaching*. When these words are compounded to form the word *heterodidaskaleo*, it means *a doctrine of a different kind or a teaching of a different sort*.

The false teaching that Paul was referring to was well-packaged and sounded quite sophisticated. But it didn't match what Jesus or he and the other apostles had taught. It was *a doctrine of a different kind*. The leaders who were advocating these errors had modified the truth to accommodate the culture, which is exactly what is happening in our culture today.

They Yearned To Be Profound Professors of Scripture

When we come to First Timothy 1:7, Paul explained what he understood to be the desire of these teachers' hearts. He said, "Desiring to be teachers of the law; understanding neither what they say, nor whereof they affirm."

The word "desiring" in this verse is significant. It is the Greek word *thelo*, which means *to earnestly desire; to long for*. In this verse, *the tense depicts an earnest, ongoing desire*. These individuals were earnestly longing to be "teachers of the law," which in the Greek is the word *nomodidaskalos*. It is a compound of the words *nomos* and *didaskalos*. The word *nomos* means *rules, principles, or the unchanging and unbendable rule of faith*. The word *didaskalos* refers to *a masterful teacher; a masterful scripture-lawyer; someone scholarly in interpreting the Bible*.

Hence, these well-loved leaders had a persistent longing to handle the principles and standards of Scripture. The problem was in their understanding. The Bible says, "…Understanding neither what they say, nor whereof they affirm." The Greek word for "understanding" that Paul used here is *noountes*, and it is taken from the word *nous*, which is the word for *the mind*. It refers to *the ability to think, to reason, to understand, and to comprehend*. In this case, their "understanding" was defective because they really didn't know the Scriptures.

Being a gifted speaker with great diction and a commanding presence is wonderful, but it is not enough. Before a person begins to preach or teach the Word of God, he needs to have a solid understanding of the basics of Scripture. Trying to accurately teach the Bible without a good grasp on the ABCs of the faith would be like trying to do algebra or calculus without knowing how to add and subtract.

Hebrews 4:12 in *The Message* says God's "…powerful Word is sharp as a surgeon's scalpel, cutting through everything, whether doubt or defense, laying us open to listen and obey…." When a person teaches or preaches the Word, he is performing spiritual surgery on the hearts and souls of the listeners. Therefore, anyone who desires to handle the Word must know the basics of the faith and be properly schooled in the Scriptures. In effect, Paul said these errant teachers were making doctrinal mistakes because they had never been schooled.

The Holy Spirit Prophesied of a Departure From the Faith

Throughout the New Testament, the Holy Spirit foretold of the great deception that would come in the last days. As we have noted through this series, the apostle Paul voiced this warning in First Timothy 4:1, saying, "Now the Spirit speaketh expressly, that in the latter times some shall depart from the faith, giving heed to seducing spirits and doctrines of devils."

The phrase "speaketh expressly" is the Greek word *rhetos*, which describes *something spoken clearly, unmistakably, and vividly*. The use of this word indicates that the Spirit was speaking in the strongest and clearest language, describing *something that is unquestionable, certain, and sure*. It would take place in the "latter times."

In Greek, the word "latter" is the word *husteros*, and the word "times" is the word *kairos*. The phrase *husteros kairos* — translated here as "latter times" — means *the very ultimate end of the Church age, just before everything wraps up*. Here we see the Holy Spirit speaking through Paul in the First Century, pointing His finger 2,000 years into the future — the very season in which we are now living — and forecasting that "some shall depart from the faith."

The words "the faith" in Greek include a definite article, which means this is not just faith for signs and wonders or faith for financial breakthrough or faith for healing. This is *the* faith." It refers to *the absolute, time-tested truth of Scripture.* The Holy Spirit said a certain number of people will depart from the faith as a result of "giving heed to seducing spirits and doctrines of devils."

The Greek word translated here as "seducing" is *planao*, and it means *deception; a moral wandering.* This word depicts *a person or nation that has veered from a solid path.* What's interesting about this word is that it was also used to describe *an animal that had lost its way and could not find the path back home.* By using the word *planao*, the Spirit was prophesying that at the end of the age, some people in the Church are going to veer so far off track morally that they'll lose their way and not seem to be able to make it back.

Compromising Christians Have 'Itching Ears'

In the apostle Paul's second letter to Timothy, he continued his foretelling of the condition of the Church in the last days, saying, "For the time will come when they will not endure sound doctrine; but after their own lusts shall heap to themselves teachers, having itching ears" (2 Timothy 4:3).

The phrase "itching ears" essentially refers to people with a mindset that thinks, *I've already heard all this doctrinal teaching, and I'm tired of hearing it. It's old and outdated. I want to hear something new, something different that I've never heard before.* In the last days, there will be people in the Church with "itching ears" who will have a greater desire to hear nonsense rather than the sound doctrine of Scripture.

Paul said they shall "heap to themselves teachers." The word "heap" here describes *piles and piles.* These individuals who can no longer tolerate sound doctrine will gather together piles and piles of errant teachers who modify the truth in order to meet the demands of what people want to hear.

They Will Turn From the Truth to Fables

In verse 4, Paul went on to say, "And they shall turn away their ears from the truth, and shall be turned unto fables." The meaning of this verse is powerfully illustrated by a major shift that took place in the Russian art world after the Bolshevik Revolution in 1917.

Prior to this historical event, talented artists painted beautifully detailed artwork depicting biblical truth. Illustrated paintings from Scripture adorned the walls of churches and believers' homes all across Russia before the Bolshevik Revolution. But in 1917 when the communists came into power, their atheistic mindset purged the Russian world of all things biblical. Scriptural truth fell out of fashion, and thousands upon thousands of biblical paintings were ripped from homes and churches and destroyed.

From that time on, the same talented painters with the same incredible gifts decided to use their abilities to create magnificent illustrations of Russian fairy tales. Thus, these amazingly skilled artists went from creating exquisite works of *scriptural truth* to creating resplendent works of *fairy tales*. This parallels what Paul prophesied many end-time believers would do at the end of the age. The truth of God's Word would fall out of fashion and be exchanged for fables.

Make no mistake. Demonic spirits are the cause for this departure from the truth. Satan hates the truth, and he is doing everything he can to sanitize it from society. He wants it thrown away or placed out of sight because it is a threat to his kingdom. He loves "progressive thinkers" who alter the Gospel in the name of political correctness. A fairy tale may entertain you, but only the truth of Scripture can transform your life.

Friend, the decision is yours. Do you want the transforming power of the truth, or do you want fairy tales? The Bible is the most powerful and important book of all time. As pastors, teachers, and believers, our job is to present the pure truth of Scripture without modifications. Regardless of the generation we live in or societal trends, truth is always truth, and we need to make a decision that we are going to stick with the teaching of Scripture even if popular opinion says otherwise.

STUDY QUESTIONS

**Study to shew thyself approved unto God, a workman that
needeth not to be ashamed, rightly dividing the word of truth.**
— 2 Timothy 2:15

1. According to Hebrews 13:7, how does the Lord want you to treat
    your spiritual leaders? What reason does He provide? (Also *consider*
    James 3:1.)

2. There are two vital characteristics that all believers need in these last
    days — qualities you can pray and ask God to develop in you and
    your leaders. Read Proverbs 16:6; 22:4; 29:23; Matthew 18:4; and
    First Peter 5:5 and identify these life-changing characteristics and the
    blessings that accompany them.

PRACTICAL APPLICATION

**But be ye doers of the word, and not hearers only,
deceiving your own selves.**
— James 1:22

Leaders have tremendous impact. Their lives influence others even when
they are unaware of it. If they go astray from the truth of Scripture, they
will undoubtedly take others with them.

1. The truth is, everyone, including you, is leading someone. Stop and
    think: *Who am I leading? Who is looking up to me, watching my life and
    listening to my words? What kind of influence am I offering? How can I
    come up higher in my leading?*

2. How has this study helped you see and better understand the enemy's
    attack against your leaders?

3. Who do you know in leadership that you now realize you need to
    begin praying for more regularly? Take a few moments right now to
    intercede for the leaders in your life. Pray that their hearts will remain
    pure and that they will stay humbly connected with the clear truth of
    Scripture.

TOPIC

Placing a Fixed Foundation Under People's Lives

SCRIPTURES

1. **1 Timothy 4:1** — Now the Spirit speaketh expressly, that in the latter times some shall depart from the faith, giving heed to seducing spirits and doctrines of demons.

SYNOPSIS

The Temple of Serapis in the ancient city of Ephesus is certainly a magnificent site to see. Its remains, which are still visible today, demonstrate the enormous size of this once very active place of worship. For instance, the columns that once supported the building weighed about 80 tons apiece. And the pedestals upon which each of the columns sat were equally as monstrous. They had to be massive and strong in order to hold the 80-ton columns. Clearly, this temple was built to last.

Solid, stable foundations provide strength and support for us to build things on that will last. Investing time, effort, and resources in building your foundation will always pay off. This is not only true of a house or a public building — it is also true for your spiritual foundation.

The emphasis of this lesson:

People who invest time and effort building a solid spiritual foundation in the lives of others are called good ministers of Jesus Christ.

Writing under the influence of the Holy Spirit, the apostle Paul said, "Now the Spirit speaketh expressly, that in the latter times some shall depart from the faith, giving heed to seducing spirits, and doctrines of devils" (1 Timothy 4:1). This verse is so foundational to this series, we are going to quickly review its meaning once again.

The Holy Spirit Said, 'This Is Definitely Going To Happen!'

In this passage, it is almost as if the Spirit of God is reaching through the pages of the Bible to grab us and wake us to make sure we truly grasp what He's saying. As we have noted, the phrase "speaketh expressly" is the Greek word *rhetos*, and it describes *something that is absolutely clear and unmistakable*. The Spirit is speaking and declaring emphatically that something categorical is going to take place, and it cannot be stopped.

This portion of the verse could be translated as, *"Now the Spirit speaks in the strongest and clearest of language; He speaks in undeniable, unmistakable terms."* Through Paul, the Holy Spirit points a prophetic finger 2,000 years into the future and proclaims, "...In the latter times some shall depart from the faith."

It Will Occur in the 'Latter Times'

The word "latter" is the Greek word *husteros*, which describes *the very ultimate end of a thing when nothing more is left over*. And the word "times" is the Greek word *kairos*, which describes *a season*. When these two words are put together to form "latter times" (*husteros kairos*), it describes *the very last season of the Church age with no more seasons after it*.

Interestingly, in Matthew 24, Jesus gave His disciples a long list of signs that would mark the end of the age and His return, and the very first sign He gave was *the presence of worldwide deception*. Jesus said deception would be so prolific that even some who are saved will be taken captive by it.

Therefore, we need to take to heart the Holy Spirit's warning in First Timothy 4:1 and know that He is not trying to scare us; He's trying to *prepare* us. We are now living in this final season — the "latter times" — and the Lord doesn't want us to be infected by the spirit of this age. He wants us to guard against deception by staying grounded in the truth.

What This Departure Will Look Like

Returning to our foundational verse in First Timothy 4:1, the Holy Spirit declared emphatically that in the latter times, "...some shall depart from the faith." The word "depart" here is the Greek word *aphistemi*, which means *to stand apart from; to distance one's self from; to step away from*. This word describes *a very gradual withdrawal from something.* In the context of this verse, *it is a very slow, almost imperceptible move away from the time-tested truth of Scripture.* It is from this very Greek word that we derive the word "apostate" or "apostasy."

This departure is not only from the faith. It is also a gradual modification of previously established standards. Things that people in society once believed were wrong slowly become accepted. The reason for this is a result of them "…giving heed to seducing spirits and doctrines of devils." The phrase "giving heed" in Greek is the word *prosecho,* and it means *to embrace.* As people depart from the solid truth of God's Word, they will begin to embrace new ideas and concepts not in line with Scripture.

Seducing Spirits Are Influencing the Departure

The unseen force behind this withdrawal is "seducing spirits and doctrines of devils." The word "seducing" is the Greek word *planao,* which means *to wander off course.* This tells us the aim of these evil spirits: to lead people off course. The word *planao* depicts *a person (or nation) that has veered from a solid path.* This passage suggests a moral wandering on a worldwide scale that will occur at the very end of the age.

This word *planao* — translated here as "seducing" — depicts the behavior of someone who once walked on a solid path but is now drifting and teetering on the edge of a treacherous route. This person has either already departed from the solid path and lost his bearings, or he is currently in the process of departing and is likely unaware of it.

The word "seducing" also indicates a person is going cross-grain against all that was once a part of his core belief system. Sadly, he is now deviating from his former, solid, moral position and embracing a course that is unreliable, unpredictable, and dangerous. There will be a mass divergence of this nature that will take place at the end of the age.

How Should We Respond to Paul's Warning?

Clearly, Paul wrote these warnings to Timothy to urge him to take action by bringing correction to the leaders who had already veered off course. He also gave Timothy — and us — clear instruction as how we are to respond to this situation. He said, "If thou put the brethren in remembrance of these things, thou shalt be a good minister of Jesus Christ, nourished up in the words of faith and of good doctrine, whereunto thou hast attained" (1 Timothy 4:6).

To understand this passage, we need to understand the meaning of the word "remembrance." This is the Greek word *hupotithemi*. It is a compound of the words *hupo* and *tithemi*. The word *hupo* means *by or under*; the word *tithemi* means *to lay, place, or position something, like a foundation*. Because *tithemi* carries an architectural concept, it can picture *one laying a foundation underneath the brethren*.

Hence, Paul said to Timothy and to all believers, "If you want to be a good minister of Jesus Christ, you have to be actively involved in establishing a solid foundation underneath other people's lives." This is what it means to put the brethren *in remembrance*.

Remember, foundations are extremely important. People need something strong, solid, and reliable upon which they can build their lives. If you really want to please Jesus, deal in truth. Focus on building a good spiritual foundation in other people's lives — one that's not cracked, shaky, or shifting. Give them the solid truth of Scripture, not a modified version. This will make you a good minister of Jesus Christ. It is the answer to dealing with seducing spirits and doctrines of devils.

STUDY QUESTIONS

Study to shew thyself approved unto God, a workman that needeth not to be ashamed, rightly dividing the word of truth.
— 2 Timothy 2:15

Jesus recognized the vital importance of the proper foundation in our lives through His parable of the wise and foolish builders. Carefully contemplate this story recorded in Matthew 7:24-27 (also *see* Luke 6:46-49) and answer these questions.

1. Which of these builders heard the life-giving words of Jesus?
2. Which of these builders experienced the rain, winds, and flood?
3. What is the major difference between the two kinds of builders — what sets them apart?
4. What is the Holy Spirit showing you in this parable that you can apply in your own life?

PRACTICAL APPLICATION

> But be ye doers of the word, and not hearers only,
> deceiving your own selves.
> — James 1:22

The Bible says, "If you want to be a good minister of Jesus Christ, you must be actively involved in establishing a solid foundation underneath other people's lives."

1. Stop and think: Who has God placed in *your* life — past or present — to help you build a sturdy foundation of faith? What specific things did they do to establish you on solid ground?

2. In whose life are you presently working to build a strong foundation of faith? What specifically are you doing to bring it about?

LESSON 13

TOPIC

How To Be a Good Minister of Jesus Christ

SCRIPTURES

1. **1 Timothy 4:1** — Now the Spirit speaketh expressly, that in the latter times some shall depart from the faith, giving heed to seducing spirits and doctrines of demons.

2. **1 Timothy 4:6** — If thou put the brethren in remembrance of these things, thou shalt be a good minister of Jesus Christ, nourished up in the words of faith and of good doctrine, whereunto thou hast attained.

GREEK WORDS

1. "remembrance" — ὑποτίθημι (*hupotithemi*): a compound of ὑπο (*hupo*) and τίθημι (*tithemi*); the word ὑπο (*hupo*) means by or under; τίθημι (*tithemi*) means to lay, place, or position something, like a foundation; because τίθημι (*tithemi*) carries an architectural concept, it can picture one laying a foundation underneath the brethren

2. "thou shalt be" — ἔση (*ese*): the future tense of εἰμί; you will become; this will make you to be

3. "good" — καλός (*kalos*): good or useful; can refer to that which is outwardly attractive or to what is inwardly noble; frequently used to denote good, noble actions or superior behavior; pictures something that is exceptional, of the highest quality, outstanding, or superb; handsome, elegant, suitable

4. "minister" — διάκονος (*diakonos*): a high-level servant; a sophisticated and highly trained servant who served the needs of others; a servant whose primary responsibility was to serve food and wait on tables; a waiter who painstakingly attends to the needs, wishes, and desires of his or her client; pictured serving that was honorable, pleasurable, and done in a fashion that made people being served as if they were nobility

5. "servant" — δοῦλος (*doulos*): the most abject term for a slave in the New Testament; it depicts one totally sold into slavery; a slave for life; one who was perpetually bound to do the bidding of his owner; a slave whose principle task is to fulfill the desires of his master for the rest of his life; to help, assist, and fulfill his master's wants and dreams to the exclusion of all else; this servant's existence was to service his master in whatever way the master asked or demanded; it is the picture of one whose will is completely swallowed up in the will of another

6. "minister" — ὑπηρέτης (*huperetes*): a class of criminals that were so low, so detestable, and so contemptible that they were outcast, removed from society, and placed into the bottom galleys of huge ships, where they literally became the engines of ships; they endlessly rowed and kept the ship moving forward; can be translated minister, servant, or under-rower to depict individuals who keep things moving; was used to describe an official in a synagogue whose function was to keep things moving; could also describe an assistant or one whose will is to fulfill the purpose of his master

7. "of Jesus Christ" — Χριστοῦ Ἰησοῦ (*Christou Iesou*): of Christ Jesus; like Christ Jesus

SYNOPSIS

As noted in our last lesson, the Temple of Serapis was located in the city of Ephesus and it was massive in size. The fact that there was such an elaborate shrine to this Egyptian religion testifies of the very large enclave of Egyptians living in Ephesus at that time. History documents that when Arsinoe, the sister of Cleopatra, ran for her life, she took refuge in the city of Ephesus until she was eventually found and assassinated by her sister.

Not only were the Egyptians in Ephesus great in number, but they were also great in wealth. Hence, they constructed the lavish Temple of Serapis and carried out their dark, sinister religious practices, including all kinds of debauchery and sexual immorality. Being a pagan city, Ephesus was host to perverse activities occurring everywhere. This presented a great temptation for new believers who had just been delivered from that lifestyle.

To help Christians overcome all the sights and sounds of the pagan practices trying to pull them back into past sinful patterns, the apostle Paul told Timothy to begin building a strong spiritual foundation under them. Working to establish them in the faith would make Timothy a good minister of Jesus Christ.

The emphasis of this lesson:

When we come under fellow believers with the Word of God and lay a solid foundation of truth to undergird them, God sees us as good ministers of Jesus Christ, and it pleases Him.

In First Timothy 4:1, the apostle Paul said, "Now the Spirit speaketh expressly, that in the latter times some shall depart from the faith, giving heed to seducing spirits and doctrines of demons." When you read this verse of Scripture in the Greek, you see that the Holy Spirit is speaking very strongly. In fact, He is speaking so emphatically, it is as if He is reaching through the pages of the New Testament to shake us and wake us to make sure we hear what He is saying.

The phrase **"speaketh expressly"** is the Greek word *rhetos*, which describes *something that is emphatic, categorical, and will definitely and most assuredly come to pass — there is no stopping it from happening.* What did the Holy Spirit so ardently warn us would be coming in the last days? He said that some would depart from the faith.

We have noted that when Paul wrote this during the First Century, the Church was already dealing with an attack against the Gospel. Well-known and highly respected spiritual leaders had begun making modifications to the truth, and it was leading people astray. Yet comparatively speaking, the

Holy Spirit forecasted that in the latter times — which means at the very ultimate end of the Church age — there would be a departure from the faith like the world had never seen.

The Greek word for **"depart"** in this verse is the word *aphistemi*, which means *to stand apart from, to distance one's self from, to step away from, to withdraw from,* or *to shrink away from.* It depicts *a departure that takes place very slowly over a long period of time.* In context, it is *a little-by-little backing away from the faith that what was once believed, cherished, and adhered to,* "giving heed" to something very different.

The phrase **"giving heed"** is the Greek word *prosecho*, which means *leaning toward something to embrace it.* Those "departing" and "giving heed" would be gradually backing away from the time-tested teaching of the Bible to embrace new ideas, new concepts, and new cultural norms that are not in sync with Scripture. This deviant exchange is the activity of "seducing spirits and doctrines of devils."

The word **"seducing"** is the Greek word *planao*, and it describes *deception or a moral wandering.* It depicts *a person or nation that has veered from a solid path.* In the last days, false teaching will become so deceptive and so prevalent, it will cause people to morally and spiritually lose their bearings.

In addition to "seducing spirits" leading people astray, the Bible says there will also be "doctrines of demons" at work. The word **"doctrines"** in Greek is the word *didaskalia*, and it describes *well-packaged teaching, new systems of thought, new philosophies, and new ideas that are modifications of the truth.* The Holy Spirit forecasted through Paul that at the very outer edge of the end of time, people in the world and even in the Church would fall under demonic influence and begin distancing themselves from the truth of Scripture they once believed.

We Are To Come Under Others With God's Word and Lay a Foundation

To combat the lunacy perpetuated by seducing spirits and doctrines of demons, the apostle Paul said, "If thou put the brethren in remembrance of these things, thou shalt be a good minister of Jesus Christ, nourished up in the words of faith and of good doctrine, whereunto thou hast attained" (1 Timothy 4:6).

In this verse, we are instructed to "put the brethren in remembrance of these things." As we learned in our previous lesson, the word "remembrance" is the Greek word *hupotithemi*, which is a compound of the words *hupo* and *tithemi*. The word *hupo* is a preposition, which means *to be under*; the word *tithemi* is a verb and means *to lay, place, or position something, like a foundation*. When the two words are compounded, it pictures *one laying a foundation underneath something*. In this case, it is a foundation under the brethren.

This passage could actually be translated as, "If you are in the business of building a foundation underneath your Christian brothers and sisters, thou shalt be a good minister of Jesus Christ...." The phrase "thou shalt be" in Greek is the term *ese*, which means *this qualifies you to be*. Thus, a really good minister who is a responsible believer is one who *hupo* — comes under other people's lives — and *tithemi* — puts a foundation underneath them.

When people hear the Gospel message and choose to repent of their sins and make Christ their Lord and Savior, they are immediately made a part of God's family. Yet at that moment they have no foundation of faith in their lives. In is our job as believers to see ourselves as servants and *come under* these newly saved individuals and *lay, place, or position a foundation* of the faith underneath their lives. And according to the Greek tense of the word *tithemi*, this is to be *a continuous effort*.

To be clear, the Holy Spirit's instructions through Paul are not just for pastors, Christian writers, or Bible teachers on radio and TV. They are for anyone who has influence in someone else's life. Thus, if you are a parent or grandparent with children or grandchildren, this verse is for you. If you are an employer who has employees, this verse is for you. The truth is, this verse is for everyone because all of us have a measure of influence in other people's lives. God is expecting you to *hupo* — *come under other people* — and *tithemi* — *lay a foundation of truth underneath them*.

Those who are standing on the rock-solid foundation of God's Word will be protected from wrong thinking and the delusion that is pervading the world today. The Bible will arm them with common sense and provide the discernment they need. And you are the instrument in God's hands to help bring this about.

The Actions of a Good Minister Are Outstanding

The Bible says when you come up under people and lay a foundation of faith, you will be qualified to be a "good minister of Jesus Christ." The word "good" is the Greek word *kalos*, and it describes *something good or useful*. It can refer to *that which is outwardly attractive or to what is inwardly noble*. Frequently, the word *kalos* is used to denote *good, noble actions or superior behavior*. It pictures *something that is exceptional, of the highest quality, outstanding, or superb*.

For example, imagine a person who is a connoisseur of art. He could walk through an art gallery and see many beautiful pieces of fine art. A great painting over here and a stunning statue over there, and on and on he would go, viewing the talented work of many artists. But then he comes to a particular display in the gallery that totally captures his attention. It is such a magnificent piece of art that he is seized with delight. It is not just good; it is *kalos* — the word used in First Timothy 4:6. It is superior, superb, and of the highest quality. It is so magnificent that it overshadows everything else he has seen in the gallery that day.

That is a picture of the word *kalos* — translated as "good"— used in First Timothy 4:6. This lets us know that Jesus is connoisseur of ministers. As He walks in the midst of the Church, which is what the Bible tells us He does in Revelation 1 and 2, He observes His people serving. One is ministering and serving in this area, another is ministering and serving in another area, and He is so impressed and encouraged by all who are active.

Then Jesus comes across one particular person who is "putting the brethren in remembrance" (*hupotithemi*). This believer is *hupo* — coming under the lives of others who need a foundation — and *tithemi* — laying the foundation of biblical truth they need. When Jesus sees the work of this minister, He says, "Wow! Now that is spectacular. Everything I've seen is good, but this is just outstanding, magnificent, and superb. This person is an exceptional and outstanding (*kalos*) minister of Jesus Christ."

We Are All 'Servants' and 'Minsters' of Jesus Christ

Those who humbly serve others by laying a foundation of the faith under them are called "good ministers of Jesus Christ" (1 Timothy 4:1). We have seen what the word "good" means. Now let's look at the meaning of the word "minister." In the New Testament, there are three Greek words used to describe all believers.

The first Greek word is *doulos*. It is often translated as "servant," as we are all *servants of Jesus Christ*. The word *doulos* is *the most abject term for a slave in the New Testament*. It depicts *one totally sold into slavery; a slave for life; one who was perpetually bound to do the bidding of his owner; a slave whose principle task is to fulfill the desires of his master for the rest of his life — to help, assist, and fulfill his master's wants and dreams to the exclusion of all else*. This servant's existence was to service his master in whatever way the master asked or demanded. It is the picture of *one whose will is completely swallowed up in the will of another*. James 1:1 is an example of this usage.

The second Greek word is *huperetas*. It is often translated as "minister," which is what we find in First Corinthians 4:1 when the apostle Paul said, "Let a man so account of us, as of the *ministers* of Christ, and stewards of the mysteries of God." The word *huperetas* — translated here as "ministers" — described *a class of criminals that were so low, so detestable, and so contemptible that they were outcast, removed from society, and placed into the bottom galleys of huge ships, where they literally became the engines of ships*. These under-rowers endlessly rowed and kept the ship moving forward. The word *huperetas* can be translated *minister, servant, or under-rower to depict individuals who keep things moving*. This term was used to describe *an official in a synagogue whose function was to keep things moving*.

As "ministers" (*huperetas*), we are called to be under-rowers who keep the Kingdom of God moving forward. We are to be committed to where God called us to be. This term describes all believers who serve Christ.

The third Greek word used to describe believers is *diakonos*. This is the word we find in First Timothy 4:6, which is translated as "minister." The word *diakonos* was used in very wealthy homes in the First Century to describe *a high-level servant; a sophisticated and highly trained servant who served the needs of others; a servant whose primary responsibility was to serve food and wait on tables*. The word *diakonos* describes *a waiter who painstakingly attends to the needs, wishes, and desires of his or her client*. It pictured serving that was *honorable, pleasurable, and done in a fashion that made people being served as if they were nobility*.

The fact that the Holy Spirit chose to use the word *diakonos* in First Timothy 4:6 tells us that in order to be "good ministers," God expects us to serve good *spiritual* food, and we are to do it honorably, pleasurably, and professionally. We are to handle ourselves in such a way that those we are serving feel like nobility. And as servers, we are to know with certainty that the food we are serving is of the highest quality and safe for consumption. In other words, we are to provide solid biblical teaching that people can trust — teaching they need to build a strong foundation in the faith and be healthy spiritually. It is this kind of serving that qualifies you as a good minister of Jesus Christ.

STUDY QUESTIONS

Study to shew thyself approved unto God, a workman that needeth not to be ashamed, rightly dividing the word of truth.
— 2 Timothy 2:15

1. The Holy Spirit uses three Greek words throughout the New Testament to describe all believers. Carefully review these words and their meanings. Of the three, which do you personally identify with most? Why?
2. In Jeremiah 6:16 (*GOD'S WORD*), the Lord spoke to the prophet and told him to tell the people of Israel, "This is what the Lord says: Stand at the crossroads and look. Ask which paths are the old, reliable paths. Ask which way leads to blessings. Live that way, and find a resting place for yourselves...." Stop and think: What are some of the "old, reliable paths" that you know? What are some practical ways to walk these out?

PRACTICAL APPLICATION

But be ye doers of the word, and not hearers only, deceiving your own selves.
— James 1:22

Knowing that the devil is sly, subtle, and extremely deceptive in his ways, it is a good practice to stop and check your spiritual vital signs every now and then to make sure seducing spirits and doctrines of devils are not influencing your life.

1. Be honest. Do you believe the same biblical truths you believed five years ago? Ten years ago? Twenty years ago? If not, why?

2. Have the principles of God's Word become watered down by the enemy's deceptions? Or have they become clearer and more powerful in your life?

3. In your own words, briefly describe how your faith has changed over the past few years (how is your knowledge of Scripture, your understanding of who God is, and your perception of who you are in Christ different).

LESSON 14

TOPIC

The Right Spiritual Diet

SCRIPTURES

1. **1 Timothy 4:1** — Now the Spirit speaketh expressly, that in the latter times some shall depart from the faith, giving heed to seducing spirits and doctrines of demons.

2. **1 Timothy 4:6** — If thou put the brethren in remembrance of these things, thou shalt be a good minister of Jesus Christ, nourished up in the words of faith and of good doctrine, whereunto thou hast attained.

GREEK WORDS

1. "remembrance" — ὑποτίθημι (*hupotithemi*): a compound of ὑπο (*hupo*) and τίθημι (*tithemi*); the word ὑπο (*hupo*) means by or under; τίθημι (*tithemi*) means to lay, place, or position something, like a foundation; because τίθημι (*tithemi*) carries an architectural concept, it can picture one laying a foundation underneath the brethren

2. "thou shalt be" — ἔση (*ese*): the future tense of εἰμί; you will become; this will make you to be

3. "good" — καλός (*kalos*): good or useful; can refer to that which is outwardly attractive or inwardly noble; frequently used to denote good, noble actions or superior behavior; pictures something that exceptional, of the highest quality, outstanding, or superb; handsome, elegant, suitable

4. "minister" — διάκονος (*diakonos*): a high-level servant; a sophisticated and highly trained servant who served the needs of others; a servant whose primary responsibility was to serve food and wait on tables; a waiter who painstakingly attends to the needs, wishes, and desires of his or her client; pictured serving that was honorable, pleasurable, and done in a fashion that made people being served as if they were nobility

5. "of Jesus Christ" — Χριστοῦ Ἰησοῦ (*Christou Iesou*): of Christ Jesus; like Christ Jesus

6. "nourished up" — ἐντρέφω (*entrepho*): the tense is continuous; it means to put into the mouth to taste, digest, and incorporate into one's system; to be nourished; pictures the receiving of nourishment that strengthens the recipient; can refer to nourishment of the spirit or mind; a diet required for one to be strong and healthy

7. "of the faith" — τῆς πίστεως (*tes pisteos*): literally, of the faith or of faith

8. "good doctrine" — καλῆς διδασκαλίας (*kales didaskalias*): a compound of καλῆς (*kales*) and διδασκαλία (*didaskalia*); the word καλῆς (*kales*) is from καλός (*kalos*), and it means good or useful; can refer to that which is outwardly attractive or to what is inwardly noble; something that exceptional, of the highest quality, outstanding, or superb; διδασκαλία (*didaskalia*) means the teaching of doctrine; compounded, καλῆς διδασκαλίας (*kales didaskalias*) means beneficial, exceptional, outstanding teaching and doctrine

9. "thou hast attained" — παρακολουθέω (*parakoloutheo*): a compound of παρά (*para*) and ἀκολουθέω (*akoloutheo*); the word παρά (*para*) means alongside; ἀκολουθέω (*akoloutheo*) means to follow as an attendant; to cleave to steadfastly; to persistently give attention to and to wholeheartedly follow after; to accompany; to follow faithfully at one's side; a possible reference to following Paul

SYNOPSIS

Situated in the heart of the ancient city of Ephesus was a place known as the *agora*. This is the Greek word for "marketplace." The *agora* was a lively shopping complex filled with all sorts of foods — varieties of luscious fruits, scrumptious breads, and hearty meats. Everyone was well acquainted with the *agora*, as it was the "supermarket" of the First

Century. All that was required for a healthy, balanced diet could be found and purchased here.

Just as you need to eat right physically to maintain a healthy body, you also need to eat right spiritually to grow and maintain a healthy spirit. The apostle Paul confirmed this, saying that we are to be "…nourished up in the words of faith and of good doctrine…" (1 Timothy 4:6). *Words of faith* and *good doctrine* are two major "food groups" that nourish our spirit and soul. Sustenance from these two sources work together to provide a healthy, balanced diet that will make us strong Christians.

The emphasis of this lesson:

In order to be healthy and effective ministering servants of Jesus Christ, we must make sure we are consuming healthy spiritual food — a balance of words of faith and of good doctrine.

Our Anchor Verse Summary

In First Timothy 4:1, the Holy Spirit prophesied what is going to take place in the Church in the closing days of the Church age. Writing under the unction of the Holy Spirit, Paul said, "Now the Spirit speaketh expressly, that in the latter times some shall depart from the faith, giving heed to seducing spirits and doctrines of demons."

As we have thoroughly noted, the phrase "speaketh expressly" is from the Greek word *rhetos*, which describes *something that is undeniable, unmistakable, and categorical.* The meaning here is so clear and emphatic that there is no way it can be misconstrued. The Spirit has declared unequivocally that something will most definitely take place at the very end of the Church age — even *inside* the Church.

He said, "…In the latter times some shall depart from the faith…." Thankfully, He didn't say *everyone* would depart from the faith — just a notable *some.* The Greek meaning of the word "some" implies a significant number of people. But regardless of how many depart, you don't have to be one of them. You can keep your head on straight by staying grounded in God's Word.

When the Bible says that some will *depart* from the faith, it doesn't mean they're going to *reject* the faith. Rejecting the faith is a sudden, abrupt action. Departing from the faith is a very slow, gradual withdrawal from the truth that was once believed and cherished. Little by little, these individuals will distance themselves from sound, biblical doctrine. That is the meaning of the words "the faith." It is not faith for miracles, finances, or signs and wonders. Since the definite article is present, we know "the faith" refers to *the sound teaching of Scripture.*

In the last 100 years, there has been a very subtle drift away from the Bible, even inside the Church. In fact, many traditional denominations have departed from the faith. Although their creeds are accurate and line up with the doctrine of Scripture, their practices do not. Some even endorse and celebrate same-sex marriage, which is totally against Scripture. This is the departure that the Holy Spirit forecasted would take place at the end of the age.

As people depart from the faith, they will begin "giving heed to seducing spirits and doctrines of devils." The phrase "giving heed" is the Greek word *prosecho*, which is a compound of the word *pros* and the word *echo.* The word *pros* means *to lean toward something,* and the word *echo* means *to embrace.* Thus, this is a picture of *people that are leaning toward something new to embrace it.*

In order to embrace something new, one must release something old. Rather that contend for the faith that was entrusted to them (*see* Jude 3), there will be people who let it go to embrace the new ideas, the new philosophies, and the new modifications of truth that the culture is celebrating.

Where are these counterfeit doctrines coming from? The Holy Spirit said they come from "seducing spirits and doctrines of devils." We have seen that the Greek term for "seducing" is *planao,* and it describes *deception, delusion, or a moral wandering.* Historically, this word was used to describe *people, a city, or a nation that had veered off track morally.* In fact, they have wandered so far from the right path that now they are walking on the very edge of a dangerous cliff, teetering on the brink of total destruction. By using the word *planao,* the Spirit it telling us that society itself will veer off the track of the Bible on which they once walked.

Society will also be highly influenced by "doctrines of devils." The word "doctrines" is the Greek word *didaskalia,* and it describes *well-packaged and well-presented teaching.* These "doctrines" will be fabricated by demonic powers and disseminated to the masses via means such as the court system, the education system, and the entertainment industry. Multiple voices will resound the same message, calling everyone everywhere to *change.* "Abandon the old way of thinking," they will say, "and embrace the new, progressive way of thinking." This is what the Holy Spirit has warned us will come at the very end of the Church age, and this is exactly what we are seeing happening today.

'Put the Brethren in Remembrance'

In the midst of all the mayhem and the meltdown of morality, Christ calls His Church to action. Through the apostle Paul, the Holy Spirit said, "If thou put the brethren in remembrance of these things, thou shalt be a good minister of Jesus Christ, nourished up in the words of faith and of good doctrine, whereunto thou hast attained" (1 Timothy 4:6).

As we learned in our previous lesson, the phrase "put the brethren in remembrance" is very significant in the Greek. The word "remembrance" is the Greek word *hupotithemi*, which is a compound of the words *hupo* and *tithemi*. The word *hupo* means *by or under*; the word *tithemi* means *to lay, place, or position something, like a foundation*. When you compound these two words to form *hupotithemi*, it depicts *a person who places a good foundation underneath other people's lives*.

In the final hour in which we live, people desperately need a solid biblical foundation on which to stand. There are many believers in the Church today who are biblically illiterate. They simply don't know what the Bible says, and the primary reason is that Scripture is no longer being taught verse-by-verse. There are many great motivational messages and much energetic preaching permeating the atmosphere of our churches, and there is certainly a place for that. But what we really need is solid scriptural teaching that helps lay a foundation of truth on which people can build their lives.

When people come to Christ and experience salvation, they come just as they are. They bring their messy lives and their unrenewed minds right into their relationship with Jesus. Although their spirit is totally made new, their soul still bears the scars of their previous life of sin. Time in the Word and the presence of the Holy Spirit is needed to transform them into the likeness of Jesus.

If we are going to be responsible believers, caring parents, and faithful friends, we are going to do what the Holy Spirit has instructed us to do — "put the brethren in remembrance of these things" — *hupotithemi.* We are going to come under people (*hupo*) and place a foundation of truth underneath them (*tithemi*). When we do this, God says it qualifies us to be a good minister of Jesus Christ.

What It Means To Be a 'Good Minister'

As God's children, our heart's desire should be to please Him. Being a "good minister" is definitely pleasing to the Lord. In First Timothy 4:6, the word "good" is the Greek word *kalos*, which means *good or useful*. It is frequently used to denote *good, noble actions or superior behavior*. It pictures something that is *exceptional, of the highest quality, outstanding, superb, handsome, elegant, or suitable*.

The word "minister" in this same verse is the Greek word *diakonos*, and it describes *a high-level servant; a servant whose primary responsibility was to serve food and wait on tables*. The word *diakonos* depicts *a waiter who painstakingly attends to the needs, wishes, and desires of his or her client*. It pictures serving that is *honorable, pleasurable, and done in a fashion that makes the people being served feel as if they are nobility*.

Furthermore, the phrase "of Jesus Christ" means *just like Jesus Christ*. When Jesus came and gave His life on the Cross, He placed a foundation underneath the Church. In the same way, when we invest our talents, time, finances, and energy to help establish a foundation of truth in other people's lives, we are acting *just like Jesus*.

Are You 'Nourished Up'?

Returning to First Timothy 4:6, we read, "If thou put the brethren in remembrance of these things, thou shalt be a good minister of Jesus Christ, nourished up in the words of faith and of good doctrine, where-unto thou hast attained."

The phrase "nourished up" in Greek is derived from the word *entrepho*, which means *to ingest; to put into the mouth to taste, digest, and incorporate into one's system*. It pictures *the receiving of nourishment that strengthens the recipient*, and it can also refer to *nourishment of the spirit or mind; a diet required for one to be strong and healthy*. Interestingly, the tense here is continuous, which means "nourished up" is something we are to do continuously.

In light of this definition, the apostle Paul — speaking under the inspiration of the Holy Spirit to Timothy and to us — said, "If you're going to be a believer that really brings Jesus pleasure and is successful in these Last Days, you're going to have to make sure you're eating the right things. You have to be nourished up, ingesting words of faith and good doctrine."

Words of Faith and of Good Doctrine

The two basic food groups from which we are to be "nourished up" are "words of faith" and "good doctrine." Words of faith teach us how to experience victory in our lives. They cover a broad spectrum of subjects and make us shout and jump for joy. They declare, "…Greater is he that is in you, than he that is in the world" (1 John 4:4) and that "…we are more than conquerors through him that loved us" (Romans 8:37). Words of faith empower us to receive supernatural healing in our body, breakthrough in our finances and relationships, and divine favor. They are encouraging, motivating, and energizing. We need these soul-stirring messages as a part of our spiritual diet.

In addition to words of faith, we also need "good doctrine." In Greek, the words "good doctrine" is a compound of *kales* and *didaskalia*. The word *kales* is from *kalos*, and it means *good or useful*. It can refer to *that which is outwardly attractive or to what is inwardly noble; something that is exceptional, of the highest quality, outstanding, or superb*. The word *didaskalia* means *the teaching of doctrine*. When these two words are compounded (*kales didaskalias*), it means *beneficial, exceptional, outstanding teaching and doctrine*.

If all you hear are *words of faith*, your spirit will be malnourished. You also need the verse-by-verse teaching of *good doctrine*. The Bible is timeless in its message, speaking relevant wisdom regarding every situation in life you will ever face. A daily soaking in the Scriptures purifies and renews your mind to think the way God thinks. So receive all the words of faith you can along with a steady consumption of good doctrine. These will make you strong and mature, and will adequately prepare you to help others.

You Will Replicate Who You're Close To

The apostle Paul wrapped up First Timothy 4:6 with the words, "whereunto thou hast attained." This phrase is very interesting. In Greek, the words "thou hast attained" is the word *parakoloutheo*. It is a compound of the word *para* and the word *akoloutheo*. The word *para* means *alongside*, and the word *akoloutheo* means *to follow as an attendant; to cleave to steadfastly;*

to persistently give attention to and to wholeheartedly follow after; to accompany; to follow faithfully at one's side with the goal of replication.

The word *parakoloutheo* is likely a reference to Timothy following Paul and his teaching, which he most certainly had heard. In fact, the phrase "words of faith and of good doctrine, whereunto thou hast attained" could literally be translated, "words of faith and the exceptional, outstanding teaching and doctrine that you have heard and received and done your best to replicate as you have followed alongside me."

Timothy had been close enough (*para*) to Paul that he could persistently give attention to and wholeheartedly follow after (*akoloutheo*) the superb words of faith and good doctrine he had heard from him.

Friend, it is important to know who you are following and consider the outcome of their life. What kind of fruit is their teaching producing in their own lives? Is it a healthy balance of *words of faith* and *good doctrine*? Do you desire to duplicate in your life and family what you see in theirs? If not, then you need to make some changes to make sure you are feeding yourself the right spiritual diet.

STUDY QUESTIONS

Study to shew thyself approved unto God, a workman that needeth not to be ashamed, rightly dividing the word of truth.
— 2 Timothy 2:15

When King Nebuchadnezzar of Babylon conquered Israel, he took Daniel, Shadrach, Meshach, and Abed-nego into his palace where he required them to eat the same foods everyone else was eating. Carefully read this account in Daniel 1:5-20.

1. What decision did Daniel make in his heart regarding the king's prescribed diet (*see* verse 8)?

2. What request did Daniel make of the king's chief servant who was taking care of their needs (*see* verses 11-13)?

3. What was the outcome of Daniel and his friends abstaining from the food everyone else was eating (*see* verses 14-20)?

4. What spiritual lessons can you learn from this real-life story and apply in your life regarding your spiritual diet?

PRACTICAL APPLICATION

But be ye doers of the word, and not hearers only,
deceiving your own selves.
— James 1:22

Hebrews 13:7 says, "Remember them which have the rule over you, who have spoken unto you the word of God: whose faith follow, considering the end of their conversation." The phrase "considering the end of their conversation" means to carefully look at their lives and consider the outcome their teaching is producing.

1. Who are you following — who is speaking God's Word into your life on a regular basis?

2. How would you describe their teaching/preaching? Does it fall in the category of "words of faith" or "good doctrine," or is it a balance of both?

3. Take a close look at these ministers and teachers and "consider their end." What kind of fruit is their teaching producing in their lives and their relationships?

4. Do you want to see these same behaviors, attitudes, and outcomes in your own life? If not, what adjustments do you need to make?

LESSON 15

TOPIC

Old Wives Tales and Fables

SCRIPTURES

1. **1 Timothy 4:1** — Now the Spirit speaketh expressly, that in the latter times some shall depart from the faith, giving heed to seducing spirits and doctrines of demons.

2. **1 Timothy 4:6,7** — If thou put the brethren in remembrance of these things, thou shalt be a good minister of Jesus Christ, nourished up in the words of faith and of good doctrine, whereunto thou hast attained. But refuse profane and old wives' fables, and exercise thyself rather unto godliness.

GREEK WORDS

1. "remembrance" — ὑποτίθημι (*hupotithemi*): a compound of ὑπο (*hupo*) and τίθημι (*tithemi*); the word ὑπο (*hupo*) means by or under; τίθημι (*tithemi*)means to lay, place, or position something, like a foundation; because τίθημι (*tithemi*) carries an architectural concept, it can picture one laying a foundation underneath the brethren

2. "minister" — διάκονος (*diakonos*): a high-level servant; a sophisticated and highly trained servant who served the needs of others; a servant whose primary responsibility was to serve food and wait on tables; a waiter who painstakingly attends to the needs, wishes, and desires of his or her client; pictured serving that was honorable, pleasurable, and done in a fashion that made people being served as if they were nobility

3. "of Jesus Christ" — Χριστοῦ Ἰησοῦ (*Christou Iesou*): of Christ Jesus; like Christ Jesus

4. "nourished up" — ἐντρέφω (*entrepho*): the tense is continuous; it means to put into the mouth to taste, digest, and incorporate into one's system; to be nourished; pictures the receiving of nourishment that strengthens the recipient; can refer to nourishment of the spirit or mind; a diet required for one to be strong and healthy

5. "of the faith" — τῆς πίστεως (*tes pisteos*): literally, of the faith or of faith

6. "good doctrine" — καλῆς διδασκαλίας (*kales didaskalias*): a compound of καλῆς (*kales*) and διδασκαλία (*didaskalia*); the word καλῆς (*kales*) is from καλός (*kalos*), and it means good or useful; can refer to that which is outwardly attractive or to what is inwardly noble; something that exceptional, of the highest quality, outstanding, or superb; διδασκαλία (*didaskalia*) means the teaching of doctrine; compounded, καλῆς διδασκαλίας (*kales didaskalias*) means beneficial, exceptional, outstanding teaching and doctrine

7. "attained" — παρακολουθέω (*parakoloutheo*): a compound of παρά (*para*) and ἀκολουθέω (*akoloutheo*); the word παρά (*para*) means alongside; ἀκολουθέω (*akoloutheo*) means to follow as an attendant; to cleave to steadfastly; to persistently give attention to and to wholeheartedly follow after

8. "refuse" — παραιτέομαι (*paraiteomai*): to reject, refuse, decline, snub, avoid, avert; to decisively turn away from; denotes the attitude of one who is so disgusted with something that he has resolved he will have

nothing to do with it; pictures one who shuns, averts, avoids, declines and rejects any form of participation in something

9. "profane" — βέβηλος (*bebelos*): signifies something so nasty that it shouldn't be permitted inside a person's home; even used to describe manure; used among Greeks to describe one who crossed a threshold without permission or an improper entrance into another realm

10. "old wives tales" — γραώδεις μύθους (*graodeis muthous*): from γραώδης (*graodes*), meaning old-womanish or senile; and μῦθος (*muthos*), meaning a myth or fantasy; stories that are told in replacement of truth; combined, typically depicts false accounts or unsubstantiated tales that are perpetrated in place of truth; used in one phrase, it means nonsensical and untrustworthy ideas produced by defective thinkers

11. "exercise" — γυμνάζω (*gumnadzo*): to exercise or train naked; used to portray naked athletes who exercised, trained, and prepared for competition in the athletic games of the ancient world; removing one's clothes was deemed necessary to eliminate all hindrances that otherwise could impede an athlete's movements; it is where we get the word "gymnasium"

12. "godliness" — εὐσέβεια (*eusebeia*): a serious commitment; a radical, fanatical devotion; a life of reverence and seriousness

SYNOPSIS

In addition to the Temple of Serapis, the School of Tyrannas, and the agora, the city of Ephesus also boasted two very large gymnasiums. Interestingly, the word "gymnasium" in Greek is the word *gumnadzo*, which means *to exercise while naked*. When athletes came to the gymnasium, they would strip themselves of all their clothing and then commence exercising with all their might.

This helps illustrate the meaning of the apostle Paul's instructions to us in First Timothy 4:7. He said, "But refuse profane and old wives' fables, and *exercise* thyself rather unto godliness." The word "exercise" in this verse is the same Greek word for gymnasium — *gumnadzo*. By using this word, the Holy Spirit is telling us to strip off everything that would hinder us in our walk with God, and become radically committed to the cause of Christ.

The emphasis of this lesson:

To keep your head on straight in a world that has gone crazy, you must recognize and reject the nonsense of old wives' fables and focus on consuming the right spiritual diet.

One Last Look at First Timothy 4:1

Writing under the inspiration of the Holy Spirit, the apostle Paul said, "Now the Spirit speaketh expressly, that in the latter times some shall depart from the faith, giving heed to seducing spirits and doctrines of demons."

Notice the first word in this verse — the word "now." When Paul says "Now," it's the equivalent of him saying, "Now hear this! I really want you to listen to what I'm about to say as the Spirit speaketh expressly." The words "speaketh expressly" is the Greek word *rhetos*, and it describes *something that is categorically going to take place*. In the strongest, clearest language, we are told *something unmistakable is going to happen that cannot be altered — not even by our prayers. It is going to happen whether we like it or not.*

The Spirit said, "...In the latter times some shall depart from the faith...." The word "latter" is the Greek word *husteros*, and it describes *the ultimate end of something, when nothing else is left*. In this case, it is latter "times" — the Greek word *kairos*, which means *a season*. Thus, the Holy Spirit emphatically declared that when we come to the very end of time — when there are no more seasons remaining — "some shall depart from the faith." While society itself will depart from common sense in the last days, this particular verse is referring to a departure from the faith by those *inside* the Church.

As a notable number of believers gradually withdraw from "the faith," which is the time-tested truth of Scripture, they will begin "giving heed to seducing spirits and doctrines of devils." The phrase "giving heed" is the Greek word *prosecho*. It is a compound of the word *pros*, which means *to lean toward something*, and the word *echo*, which means *to embrace*. As these individuals drift from the faith and release the pure Word of God they once believed and cherished, they will lean toward and begin embracing new ideas, new philosophies, and new modifications of the truth.

Jude saw this departure beginning to take place in the First Century just after the Church was birthed. That is why, instead of discussing salvation, he urged believers to "...earnestly contend for the faith which was once

delivered unto the saints" (Jude 3). Jude's instructions apply to us as well —
we need to contend for the faith rather than release it.

The truth is, no believer would knowingly embrace an evil spirit or accept
its lies over the truth of Scripture. The problem is, theses evil spirits are
"seducing." The deception they bring is very subtle and cunning. They
slowly and methodically modify the truth, one tiny increment at a time.
This seduction is a step-by-step, day-by-day, long-term process. Just as
repeated drops of water over a long period of time can erode solid rock,
the enemy's continual bombardment of ungodly messages and images can
erode even the strongest faith if not recognized and stopped.

Along with seducing spirits, "doctrines of devils" will also be at work in
the last days. The word "doctrines" here is the Greek word *didaskalia*,
and it describes *doctrine or teaching that is sophisticated and well-packaged.*
Satan and his forces will come with the most convincing public-relations
program the world has ever seen. It will be extremely well-packaged and
fed to the public from multiple directions all at the same time. The court
system, the education system, social media, movies, and television will be
used synergistically to modify the way people think so they will accept a
new reality — a reality void of scriptural truth.

The Enemy's Ultimate Goal: Lawlessness

Jesus prophesied in Matthew 24 that the world would be a *lawless* place
before His return. The apostle Paul reaffirmed this in Second Thessalonians chapter 2. The word "lawless" in the Greek is *anomia*. It is from the
word *nomos*, which means *law.* When the letter "a" is placed in front of
a word, it is a privative that reverses the meaning or condition. In this
case, *anomia* means *without law.* It describes *the elimination of fixed moral
standards.* In other words, it will be a time when everything is in a state of
flux; truth is relative and there are no absolutes.

This is the direction in which society-at-large is heading, and it will arrive
there at the very end of the age. Once people reject the long-held standard
of Scripture, the world will enter a period where there are no fixed moral
standards. With the voice of Scripture silenced, civilization will float on
the whims of the people. The lawless society will be perfectly prepared
for the man of lawlessness to rise to power — the man prophesied as the
antichrist.

Make no mistake. There is a sinister, worldwide plan being worked by Satan and his minions. The apostle Paul called it the "mystery of iniquity" (*see* 2 Thessalonians 2:7). First Timothy 4:1 confirms it is the work of "seducing spirits and doctrines of demons." Even now they are working feverishly to worm their way into the Church and deceive God's people into departing from the faith. Therefore, we must keep our head on straight by keeping a close eye on what we are consuming spiritually.

The Ingredients of a Balanced Spiritual Diet

In First Timothy 4:6, the apostle Paul described two vital ingredients needed for a healthy spiritual diet. He said, "If thou put the brethren in remembrance of these things, thou shalt be a good minister of Jesus Christ, nourished up in the words of faith and of good doctrine, whereunto thou hast attained."

We saw in our previous lesson that the phrase "nourished up" is the Greek word *entrepho,* which means *to put into the mouth to taste, digest, and incorporate into one's system.* It pictures *the receiving of nourishment that strengthens the recipient and can refer to nourishment of the spirit or mind; a diet required for one to be strong and healthy.* The tense in the Greek here is continuous, which means we are to be nourished up continuously.

The Bible says you are to be "...nourished up in the words of faith and of good doctrine, whereunto thou hast attained." Thus a balanced spiritual diet consists of "words of faith" and "good doctrine." "Words of faith" refer to inspiring messages that stir your spirit and teach you how to live victoriously. They empower you to believe and receive supernatural healing in your body, provision in your finances, restoration in your relationships, and divine favor. These encouraging and energizing messages are a vital part of your spiritual diet.

At the same time, you also need "good doctrine," which in Greek is *kales didaskalias.* This is verse-by-verse teaching that is *exceptional, of the highest quality, outstanding, or superb.* A steady diet of this solid doctrine establishes you on a firm foundation of truth and positions you to be able to place a firm foundation underneath the lives of others. A healthy balance of "words of faith" and "good doctrine" is what you need to be a good minister of Jesus Christ.

Refuse the Nonsense That Is Masquerading as Truth

Along with the instruction to eat right spiritually, Paul added, "But refuse profane and old wives' fables, and exercise thyself rather unto godliness" (1 Timothy 4:7). First, notice the word "refuse." It is the Greek word *paraiteomai*, which means *to reject, refuse, decline, snub, avoid, avert or decisively turn away from*. It denotes *the attitude of one who is so disgusted with something that he has resolved he will have nothing to do with it*. It pictures *one who shuns, averts, avoids, declines and rejects any form of participation in something*.

Paul could not have chosen a stronger word to use here. The Holy Spirit was clearly urging Timothy — *and us* — to stay completely away from "profane and old wives' fables." The word "profane" is the Greek word *bebelos*, and it signifies *something so nasty that it shouldn't be permitted inside a person's home*. This word was even used in the First Century to describe *manure*.

Think about it. No one in his right mind would tolerate a pile of manure sitting in the middle of his living room. That person wouldn't knowingly let it cross the threshold of his house. However, if an animal had somehow made it inside and defecated on the floor, the homeowner would swiftly move to remove the manure. This is a picture of what Paul was describing. Specifically, he was saying, "Have absolutely nothing to do with the *manure* of bad teaching. Shun it, avoid it, and reject any form of participation in it. It's extremely nasty and shouldn't be allowed inside of you."

He then added "old wives' fables" to his warning. In Greek, the phrase "old wives' fables" is *graodeis muthous*, which is from the word *graodes*, meaning *old-womanish or senile*; and the word *muthos*, meaning *a myth or fantasy; stories that are told in replacement of truth*. When these two words are combined to form *graodeis muthous* — translated here as "old wives' fables" — it typically depicts *false accounts or unsubstantiated tales that are perpetrated in place of truth*. It can also mean *nonsensical and untrustworthy ideas produced by defective thinkers*.

In effect, Paul was saying, "If you allow bad teaching and untrustworthy tales perpetuated in the place of truth to come into your life, it's like allowing someone to dump a nasty pile of manure in your life. Pretty soon everything is going to begin to stink, so put a stop to before it starts." What you allow into your life will determine what you become.

Exercise Yourself Unto Godliness

Instead of accepting old wives' fables, Paul urges us to "…exercise thyself rather unto godliness" (1 Timothy 4:7). The word "exercise" in this verse is the Greek word *gumnadzo*, which means *to exercise or train naked*. It was used to portray *naked athletes who exercised, trained, and prepared for competition in the athletic games of the ancient world*. Removing one's clothes was deemed necessary to eliminate all hindrances that otherwise could impede an athlete's movements. *Gumnadzo* is where we get the word "gymnasium."

Therefore, when Paul said, "Exercise yourself unto godliness," he was imploring us to strip off everything from our lives that would hinder our spiritual growth. This includes every bad teaching that is twisted and contaminated and doesn't line up with Scripture. We are to treat it like manure and throw it out.

Once we strip ourselves of everything that is impeding our spiritual growth, we are to go after "godliness." The word "godliness" is the Greek word *eusebeia*, and it describes *a serious commitment; a radical, fanatical devotion; a life of reverence and seriousness.* Exercising yourself unto godliness positions you to become the good minister that brings Jesus Christ great pleasure (*see* 1 Timothy 4:6).

Friend, just because the world is going crazy, it doesn't mean you have to join them. You can keep your head on straight if you will hear and heed the words of the Holy Spirit through Paul. Nourish your spirit with words of faith and good doctrine. Refuse profane nonsense that is parading and masquerading as good teaching. And exercise yourself unto godliness — give yourself 100 percent to the full spiritual development to which Christ has called you. Not only will you be spiritually fit, but you will also be thoroughly equipped to place a foundation of truth under the lives of others!

STUDY QUESTIONS

> **Study to shew thyself approved unto God, a workman that needeth not to be ashamed, rightly dividing the word of truth.**
> **— 2 Timothy 2:15**

In this lesson, we learned that "exercising" (*gumnadzo*) spiritually means to strip off anything and everything that hinders your spiritual growth. This instruction is reiterated by the writer of Hebrews. Take a few moments to chew on this passage: "…Let us strip off anything that slows us down or holds us back, and especially those sins that wrap themselves so tightly around our feet and trip us up; and let us run with patience the particular race that God has set before us" (Hebrews 12:1 *TLB*).

1. What specifically is the Holy Spirit surfacing in your mind that you need to strip off?
2. Can you recognize an area in your life where your moral stance/position on an issue isn't consistent with God's Word? If so, where?
3. Pause and pray, "Holy Spirit, from where did this errant belief stem? Is there anything I'm presently doing or entertaining that is feeding this belief? Please forgive me and lead me to the scriptures that soundly refute any lies I'm believing. In Jesus' name, amen."

PRACTICAL APPLICATION

> **But be ye doers of the word, and not hearers only,**
> **deceiving your own selves.**
> **—James 1:22**

God's command to you is to exercise yourself unto godliness. This is done by feeding your spirit the pure Word of God; walking and praying in the Spirit; and obeying God's Word, doing what He says. These are the activities that will build and strengthen your spiritual muscles and give you divine wisdom and common sense to guard against the devil's deceptions in these last days.

1. Be honest. Are you actively engaged in all three of these activities?
2. If so, how are you practically walking out these pursuits?
3. Which one(s) need attention?
4. What adjustments do sense the Holy Spirit is prompting you to make to faithfully exercise yourself unto godliness?

A Prayer To Receive Salvation

If you've never received Jesus as your Savior and Lord, now is the time for you to experience the new life Jesus wants to give you! To receive God's gift of salvation that can be obtained through Jesus alone, pray this prayer from your heart:

> *Jesus, I repent of my sin and receive You as my Savior and Lord. Wash away my sin with Your precious blood and make me completely new. I thank You that my sin is removed, and Satan no longer has any right to lay claim on me. Through Your empowering grace, I faithfully promise that I will serve You as my Lord for the rest of my life.*

If you just prayed this prayer of salvation, you are born again! You are a brand-new creation in Christ! Would you please let us know of your decision by going to **renner.org/salvation**? We would love to connect with you and pray for you as you begin your new life in Christ.

Scriptures for further study: John 3:16; John 14:6; Acts 4:12; Ephesians 1:7; Hebrews 10:19,20; 1 Peter 1:18,19; Romans 10:9,10; Colossians 1:13; 2 Corinthians 5:17; Romans 6:4; 1 Peter 1:3

Notes

CLAIM YOUR FREE RESOURCE!

As a way of introducing you further to the teaching ministry of Rick Renner, we would like to send you FREE of charge his teaching, "How To Receive a Miraculous Touch From God" on CD or as an MP3 download.

In His earthly ministry, Jesus commonly healed *all* who were sick of *all* their diseases. In this profound message, learn about the manifold dimensions of Christ's wisdom, goodness, power, and love toward all humanity who came to Him in faith with their needs.

☑ **YES, I want to receive Rick Renner's monthly teaching letter!**

Simply scan the QR code to claim this resource or go to: **renner.org/claim-your-free-offer**

Connect

WITH US!

www.ingramcontent.com/pod-product-compliance
Lightning Source LLC
LaVergne TN
LVHW022323080426
835508LV00041B/2387